STANDPOINTS

STANDPOINTS

Standpoints

John L. Foster

Nelson Harrap

Thomas Nelson and Sons Ltd
Nelson House Mayfield Road
Walton-on-Thames Surrey KT12 5PL

51 York Place
Edinburgh EH1 3JD

Thomas Nelson (Hong Kong) Ltd
Toppan Building 10/F
22A Westlands Road
Quarry Bay Hong Kong

Thomas Nelson (Kenya) Ltd.
P.O. Box 18123
Nairobi Kenya

Distributed in Australia by

Thomas Nelson Australia
480 La Trobe Street
Melbourne Victoria 3000
and in Sydney, Brisbane, Adelaide and Perth

© John L. Foster 1983
First Published by Harrap Ltd 1983
Reprinted 1984
This impression Published by Thomas Nelson and Sons
Ltd 1984
Reprinted 1985
(Under ISBN 0-245-53918-2)

ISBN 0-17-444159-2
Print No. 03

All Rights Reserved. This publication is protected in
the United Kingdom by the Copyright Act 1956 and in
other countries by comparable legislation. No part of it
may be reproduced or recorded by any means without
the permission of the publisher. This prohibition
extends (with certain very limited exceptions) to
photocopying and similar processes, and written
permission to make a copy or copies must therefore be
obtained from the publisher in advance. It is advisable
to consult the publisher if there is any doubt regarding
the legality of any proposed copying.

Printed in Hong Kong

Contents

Acknowledgements ix
Preface xi

AM I O.K.?

Am I O.K.?	Fran Landesman	2
I am	L. T. Baynton	2
Disruptive Minority	Alan Gilbey	3
Westerns	Iain Crichton Smith	4
Wen I Dance	James Berry	4
Parent and Child	John Kitching	6
Why?	Fran Landesman	6
As soon as I could speak	Debbie Carnegie	7
Poem for my Sister	Liz Lochhead	7
I walked along some forgotten shore	Spike Milligan	8

CITY SCENES

Streets of Childhood	Milly Harris	10
The Mary Baker City Mix	Alex Glasgow	11
Glasgow Sonnet (iii)	Edwin Morgan	12
Visiting Belfast	Wes Magee	12
The Inner Ring Road	Stanley Cook	13
City	John Kitching	14
Autumn in the Park	John Kitching	14
Snack Bar	Stanley Cook	15
January Sales	Vernon Scannell	15
Cries of London	Wes Magee	16
Incident on the Housing Estate	Wes Magee	17
A Voice from the Inner City	Rudolph Kizerman	17

CAUSE FOR CONCERN

What's in the paper?	Iain Crichton Smith	22
Summer Song	W. W. Watt	22
Separate 'Development'	Leo Aylen	23
The Irish Jokes	Wes Magee	24
Open Heart University	Spike Milligan	24
The Fish are All Sick	Anne Stevenson	25
In the New Landscape	Bruce Dawe	25

All Animals Are Equal	James Kirkup	26
The Last Tiger	Gareth Owen	28
Market Square	David Wevill	29
The Mother	Edwin Morgan	30
Murder	Edward Lowbury	31
Euthanasia	John Kitching	31
Euthanasia	Elizabeth Jennings	32
Old Age Report	Adrian Mitchell	33

CRIME AND PUNISHMENT

Jailbird	Vernon Scannell	36
I'm no good, that's what I've been told	Roger McGough	36
Harassment	Frederick Williams	37
The Tidy Burglar	Leo Aylen	38
Parents	Julius Lester	39
The Man Inside: Poems by prisoners		
Here I am, sewing . . .	Peter D.	40
It's humans that they put in prison	Eddie S.	41
I wanted to send you roses	Paul M.	41
Do you know why you are doing it?	Alan K.	42
The Other Time	Peter Appleton	43
What's the Difference?	Laurence Lerner	44

LOVE

Loving	James Berry	48
Love	Iain Crichton Smith	48
When I phoned	R. Kingsbury	49
In the Youth Club	Iain Crichton Smith	50
A Whisper I Shout With	James Berry	50
She Said	Liz Hutchins	51
December Love	David Sutton	53
Christmas Party	Wes Magee	54
First Ice	Andrey Voznesensky	55
Our Love Now	Martyn Lowery	56
It's Over	Joan Davidson	58

OTHER PEOPLE

Labelled	Roger McGough	60
A Black Man's Song	Jimi Rand	60
The Driving Instructor	Ted Walker	61
The Man in the Street	Alan Bold	62

Mum's the Word	Alan Bold	63
Edication	Rudolph Kizerman	64
The Useless Punk Rocker	Leo Aylen	66
Song: Mad Sam	Alan Bold	67
Nock Nock Oo Nock E Nock	Jimi Rand	68
Worldwide	Fazil Hüsnü Dağlarca	70
Where the Rainbow Ends	Richard Rive	70
Janos Kovacs and Wife	Michael Perneki	71

WAR

Definition	Laurence Collinson	74
Bullets	Sipho Sepamla	74
Epitaph	Grigor Vitez	75
Notes for a Movie Script	Carl Holman	76
Kill the Children	James Simmons	76
No Surrender!	Wes Magee	77
Bomb	Timothy Palmer	78
There Was a Planet	faye hoban	79
'If You Envisage Nuclear War'	Gary Scott	80
No More Hiroshimas	James Kirkup	80
Open Day at Porton	Adrian Mitchell	81
The Choice	Robert Morgan	82

THE WORLD OF WORK

School Taught Me	Leon Rosselson	84
Interview	Iain Crichton Smith	84
Time to Work	Alan Sillitoe	85
Reverie for a Secretary	Stella Coulson	87
A Working Mum	Sally Flood	88
A Bad Mistake	Gregory Harrison	90
The Presentation	Ripyard Cuddling	91
My Dad	Iain Crichton Smith	92
Unemployable	Gareth Owen	92
Redundant	Alf Money	92

REFLECTIONS

Back in the Playground Blues	Adrian Mitchell	96
Money	Carl Sandburg	97
Fantasy of an African Boy	James Berry	97
Life Insurance	Edward Lowbury	98
The Unbeliever	Edward Lowbury	99
Zen Legend	James Kirkup	100

The Not-So-Good Earth	Bruce Dawe	101
The Sensitive Philanthropist	D. J. Enright	101
Democracy	Langston Hughes	102
A Wish	Sipho Sepamla	103
Notes		105
Index of Authors		116

Acknowledgements

For permission to publish copyright material in this anthology, acknowledgement is made to the following:

To Leo Aylen for *Separate 'Development'* (published in *Return to Zululand* by Leo Aylen, published by Sidgwick & Jackson), *The Tidy Burglar* and *The Useless Punk Rocker*. To James Berry for *A Whisper I Shout With*, *Fantasy of an African Boy*, *Loving* and *Wen I Dance*. To Alan Bold for *Mum's the Word*. To Alan Bold and Borderline Press for *Man in the Street* and *Song: Mad Sam*. To Debbie Carnegie for *As soon as I could speak*. To Stanley Cook for *The Inner City Road* and *Snack Bar*. To Iain Crichton Smith for *Interview*, *In the Youth Club*, *Love*, *My Dad*, *Westerns* and *What's in the Paper? (What's in the Paper?* is from *River, River* published by Macdonald.) To Ripyard Cuddling (Jack Davitt) for *The Presentation* (reprinted from *Shipyard Muddling* published by Strong Words, 10 Greenhaugh Road, Whitley Bay, Tyne & Wear, NE25 9HF, Price 35p). For *Worldwide* by Fazil Hüsnü Dağlarca, reprinted from *Selected Poems of Fazil Hüsnü Dağlarca*, translated by Talat Sait Halman, by permission of the University of Pittsburgh Press. To Joan Davidson for *It's Over*. To Longman Cheshire for Bruce Dawe's poems *In the New Landscape* and *The Not-so-good Earth* published in *Sometimes Gladness Collected Poems 1954–1978*. To Bolt & Watson for *The Sensitive Philanthropist* by D. J. Enright first published by Chatto & Windus in *Daughters of Earth*. To Sally Flood for *A Working Mum*. To Alan Gilbey for *Disruptive Minority*. To Robbins Music Corp. Ltd for *The Mary Baker City Mix* by Alex Glasgow reproduced by permission of EMI Music Publishing Ltd. To Gregory Harrison for *A Bad Mistake*. To faye hoban for *There Was a Planet* from *Nuclear Fragments* edited by Monica Frisch. To Alfred A Knopf, Inc, for *Democracy* by Langston Hughes. To Elizabeth Jennings for *Euthanasia*. To the Longman Group Limited for *When I 'Phoned* by R. Kingsbury from *Sunday Afternoons* by Kingsbury and O'Shea. To James Kirkup for *All Animals are Equal*. To James Kirkup and Kyoto Editions for *Zen Legend*. To James Kirkup and Oxford University Press for an extract from *No More Hiroshimas*. To John Kitching for *Autumn in the Park*, *City*, *Euthanasia* and *Parent and Child*. To Rudolph Kizerman for *A Voice from the Inner City* and *Edication*. To Fran Landesman for *Am I O.K.?* and *Why?* from *The Ballad of the Sad Young Man*. To Laurence Lerner and Chatto and Windus Ltd for *What's the Difference?* by Laurence Lerner from *Directions of Memory*. To Allison & Busby for *Search for the New Land* by Julius Lester. To Edward Lowbury for *Life Insurance*, *Murder* and *The Unbeliever*. To Wes Magee for *Christmas Party*, *Cries of London*, *Incident on the Housing Estate*, *No Surrender*, *The Irish Jokes* and *Visiting Belfast*. To A D Peters & Co Ltd for *I'm no good, that's what I've been told* by Roger McGough from *Unlucky for Some* published by Turret Books. To Spike Milligan Productions Ltd for *I walked along some forgotten shore* and *Open Heart University* from *Open Heart University* by Spike Milligan published by Michael Joseph Ltd. To Adrian Mitchell for *Old Age Report* and

Open Day at Porton from Ride the Nightmare published by Jonathan Cape Ltd. To Adrian Mitchell for Back in the Playground Blues from For Beauty Douglas published by Allison and Busby. To Alf Money for Redundant from Voices 23 (Thames T.V.). To the Carcanet Press Ltd for Glasgow Sonnets iii and The Mother from From Glasgow to Saturn by Edwin Morgan. (The Mother is not a poem standing by itself but one section of a five part poem called Stobhill which gives five different views of an abortion.) To Granada Publishing Ltd for The Choice by Robert Morgan from Frontier of Living. To Gareth Owen for The Last Tiger. To Penguin Books Ltd for Unemployable by Gareth Owen from Gareth Owen: Salford Road (Kestrel Books 1979) p.60 Copyright © 1971, 1974, 1976, 1979 by Gareth Owen. To Anthony Sheil Associated Ltd for Here I am sewing by Peter D., Do you know why you are doing it? by Alan K., I wanted to send you roses by Paul M. and It's humans that they put in prison by Eddie S. from The Man Inside edited by Tony Parker. To MBA Literary Agents Ltd for A Black Man's Song and Nock Nock Oo Nock E Nock by Jimi Rand. (Nock Nock Oo Nock E Nock is published by Harrap in Bluefoot Traveller.) To Indiana University Press for Where the Rainbow Ends by Richard Rive from Poems from Black Africa edited by Langston Hughes. To Leon Rosselson for School Taught Me from That's Not The Way It's Got To Be published by Sing Publications. To Harcourt Brace Jovanovich for Money from The People, Yes by Carl Sandburg. To Vernon Scanell for Jailbird and January Sales. To Gary Scott for If you envisage Nuclear War from Nuclear Fragments edited by Monica Frish. To Rex Collins Ltd and Sipho Sepamla for A Wish and Bullets from The Soweto I Love. To Allan Sillitoe for Time to Work. To James Simmons for Kill the Children from West Strand Visions published by the Blackstaff Press, Belfast. To Oxford University Press for The Fish are All Sick from Minute by Glass Minute by Anne Stevenson. To David Higham Associates Ltd for The Driving Instructor from Collected Poems by Ted Walker. To Frederick Williams for Harrassment.

Whilst every effort has been made, we have been unable in some cases to trace the copyright holder. We should be grateful to hear from anyone who recognizes their material and who is unacknowledged. We shall be pleased to make the necessary corrections in future editions of the book.

We wish to acknowledge the following photographic sources:

Big Star Pictures: Cover photo, page 9, page 21; Chris Schwarz: page 1; Express Newspapers, photographer John Downing: page 35; Richard and Sally Greenhill: page 47; Derek Ridgers; page 59; Andrew Body: page 73; Peter Boyce: page 83; International Defence and Aid: page 95.

Preface

Standpoints is a collection of poems for teenagers to read and discuss. It consists of poems dealing with those aspects of life which are of most immediate concern to students in their last two years of compulsory schooling. In addition to their relevance, the poems have been chosen for their directness. *Standpoints* is, therefore, suitable for use with students preparing for the CSE examination or its equivalent.

Many of the poems have been published before; the remainder have been specially written for this collection. The previously published poems come from a wide variety of sources, and there are poems translated from Russian, Turkish and Hungarian, as well as works by African, American and Australian poets. As far as possible, therefore, the range of poetry in *Standpoints* reflects the universality of human experience.

The book is divided into nine sections, each containing approximately ten poems. The themes covered in these sections are: Am I O.K. ?; City Scenes; Cause for Concern; Crime and Punishment; Love; Other People; War; The World of Work; Reflections. There is a final section, consisting of brief notes on each poem. The notes provide any background information essential for an understanding of the poem, explain any significant references, and, where appropriate, suggest points for discussion.

J. L. F.

AM I O.K.?

Am I O.K.?	Fran Landesman	2
I am	L. T. Baynton	2
Disruptive Minority	Alan Gilbey	3
Westerns	Iain Crichton Smith	4
Wen I Dance	James Berry	4
Parent and Child	John Kitching	6
Why?	Fran Landesman	6
As soon as I could speak	Debbie Carnegie	7
Poem for my Sister	Liz Lochhead	7
I walked along some forgotten shore	Spike Milligan	8

Am I O.K.?

How am I?
Am I all right? Am I O.K.? Am I just too much?
How am I?
Do I make it? Do you mean it? Will you keep in touch?

How am I? On the level
Am I O.K.? Am I wunderbar?
Tell me why
Am I sunshine? Am I chocolate? Am I superstar?

How can you endure me?
I'm so insecure
When you reassure me
I just ask for more and more

Tell me now
Am I O.K.? Do you dig me? Like a breath of Spring?
Show me how
Am I solid? Am I groovy? Do I really swing?
You're a winner. You're a beauty
And I know you never lie
You're terrific. You're colossal
But, baby, how am I?
Am I O.K.?

Fran Landesman

I am

I am Tarzan, brown and loin-clothed, swinging through the trees, ape calling, rescuing at the last moment the lost hunter from the cannibals.

I am the carefree pirate on the Spanish Main leaping from the mast and fencing six men, before escaping in shark-infested water.

I am the frontier marshal, mean-faced, ruling the sidewalks with my fists of iron, shooting it out with pearl-handled colts.

I am the first English astronaut, space-walking in the velvet blackness, heading weightless towards a distant planet.

I am the tireless marathon runner, jogging through twenty six sweat-soaked miles, first into the roaring Olympic stadium.

I am the newest pop-star, roaring into the microphone, throwing off my glittering jacket, as the fans scream and wave.

I am Jimmy Brown, Class 4, slow at Maths, fair at English, must concentrate on my work.

L. T. Baynton

Disruptive Minority

Rude words on the blackboard,
Crushed chalk on the floor,
Books bunged out the window,
Run out, slam the door.

Teacher's depression
Me and my class.
Football in the playground
Connects with school glass.

Cigarettes in the toilet
And nudie books too.
When I leave this dump
Then what will I do?

I'm nothing special,
The school taught me that.
I haven't got brains
And my prospects are flat.

Can't hit back at the system
It's blank, has no features,
So while I'm at school
I'll take it out on the teachers.

Alan Gilbey

Westerns

Sometimes when I see a Western
and John Wayne rides down the street
and there's all that music
and Jack Palance stands there in his black suit
and his black hat
and he says, smiling, to John Wayne:
'Get out of town, son'

and his legs are straddled
and he's smiling
so that you can see his teeth,

sometimes I am John Wayne
and when he shoots, it's me who shoots,
and it's Hughie lying there
dead on the street.

But it never works, only for a while,
for when I see Hughie again
I don't feel like John Wayne
and he smiles at me just like Jack Palance
and I smile through my teeth.

Iain Crichton Smith

Wen I Dance

Wen I dance it noh jus
dat music swallah up mi shynis,
dat joy settle in mi eye dem,
dat swing of arm get dressed wid frill,
as timin tune up foot dem wid floor
like sey I nevva jus a-look on.

It jus dat wen I dance
o music swell up mi hearin big
an it want no knowledge,
it want no tinkin, no speakin,
all it want is feelin
well in wid swing of place movin.

Wen I dance it noh jus
dat surprise a-dictate movement,
odda rhyddm a-move my rhyddm,
I dig back to babyhood to 'member rockin,
an skippin, hoppin, runnin
all mix movement I balance in.

It jus dat wen I dance
I costumed in a rainbow mood,
I truly miself at any angle,
outfit of drums crowd mi wid madnis,
talkin Winds an string-pluckin inveigle me
an beat afta beat hot me up like sun.

Wen I dance it noh jus
dat I shif bodyweight balance
as movement a-gadda up my show,
I a-celebrate every dancer here
and no sleep can touch me now at all
an I see how I tireless.

It just dat wen I dance
I a-gadda up all mi sense dem
well in a hearin an feelin,
wid body elastic movement dem
a-tell own poetry wid every move
an man I deep in praise of all rhyddm.

James Berry

Parent and Child

I will not be what they would make me.
I will not do what they would have me do.
I will not think as they would shape me.
I will not voice what they would wish me to.

I'll be my own, I'll sing my song.
I'll touch just what I please.
I'll earn my right and learn my wrong.
My dreams will be at ease—

Unless of course it is too late
And the carving's long since done
And I cannot choose what I love and hate
For the flesh and blood is one.

John Kitching

Why?

Why is my every love a loss?
Why do our letters always cross?
Why do I always talk too much?
Why does it take so long to touch?

Why is my wisdom just a waste?
Why can't I rest alone and chaste?
Why won't I learn what time has taught?
Why am I always getting caught?

Why do I wear this foolish grin?
What would I do if I should win?
Should I be asking more or less?
Why is my every love a mess?

Fran Landesman

As soon as I could speak

As soon as I could speak—I was told to listen
As soon as I could play—they taught me to work
As soon as I found a job—I married
As soon as I married—came the children
As soon as I understood them—they left me
As soon as I had learned to live—life was gone.

Debbie Carnegie

Poem for my Sister

My little sister likes to try my shoes,
to strut in them,
admire her spindle-thin twelve-year-old legs
in this season's styles.
She says they fit her perfectly,
but wobbles
on their high heels, they're
hard to balance.

I like to watch my little sister
playing hopscotch,
admire the neat hops-and-skips of her,
their quick peck,
never-missing their mark, not
over-stepping the line.
She is competent at peever.

I try to warn my little sister
about unsuitable shoes,
point out my own distorted feet, the callouses,
odd patches of hard skin.
I should not like to see her
in *my* shoes.
I wish she could stay
sure footed,
         sensibly shod.

Liz Lochhead

I walked along some forgotten shore

I walked along some forgotten shore.
Coming the other way
      a smiling boy.
It was me.
'Who are you old man?' he said
I dare not tell him all I could say was
'Go back!'

Spike Milligan

CITY SCENES

Streets of Childhood	Milly Harris	10
The Mary Baker City Mix	Alex Glasgow	11
Glasgow Sonnet (iii)	Edwin Morgan	12
Visiting Belfast	Wes Magee	12
The Inner Ring Road	Stanley Cook	13
City	John Kitching	14
Autumn in the Park	John Kitching	14
Snack Bar	Stanley Cook	15
January Sales	Vernon Scannell	15
Cries of London	Wes Magee	16
Incident on the Housing Estate	Wes Magee	17
A Voice from the Inner City	Rudolph Kizerman	17

Streets of Childhood

Walking through the streets of childhood,
Seeing people passing by,
Now of stranger's garb and custom
Yet the same as days gone by.

Here the shops are more dejected,
Flower and Dean Street and Brick Lane
Have the same old-fashioned dwellings,
Rothschilds Building is their name.

Children playing in the courtyards,
Garbage, litter, broken stones,
Running, skipping, dodging playmates;
No green grass outside their homes.

Passing by the age-old building
Hallowed through the many years.
Praying, chanting of the rabbis
Now give way to Moslem prayers.

Tenements so overcrowded
Racial violence still is there:
But family life and faith are with them
Though they have so much to bear.

I remember Blackshirts marching
Following Mosley's creed of hate,
They threw a young girl through a window:
Death, they hoped, would be her fate.

Now the National Front is with us
Jews and blacks are spat in the face;
But when will people hear and listen
We are *all* members of the human race.

Milly Harris

The Mary Baker City Mix

Take your Mary Baker city mix and mix yourself a city to a plan,
Full of instant plastic palaces, homogenized, untouched by human hand.
Add a central plate glass precinct where pedestrians can stroll around and cry,
As they see the blackened embers of an older and much richer city die.

In the Mary Baker city mix the teak-lined supermarkets meet your eyes,
Where the open market stood you'll find the atmosphere is now deodorized,
And the bacon butty stall has disappeared and in its place you'll find a bar,
With high speed brunch and crispy lettuce you can eat from heat-sealed wrapping in your car.

In the Mary Baker city there's no place for all the buskers and the bums,
And there'll be no shuffling raincoats combing gutters for there'll be no crumbs,
Only standard issue natty gents who leave it all behind at five-fifteen,
On an air-conditioned express bus that takes 'em to some far suburban dream.

Take your Mary Baker city mix and mix yourself a city to a plan,
Take the super giant pack and make a few identicities while you can.
And as you sterilize and standardize, and cauterize the ancient city's ills,
You'll find the architects and planners have all saved themselves a cottage in the hills.

Alex Glasgow

Glasgow Sonnet (iii)

'See a tenement due for demolition?
I can get ye rooms in it, two, okay?
Seven hundred and nothin legal to pay
for it's no legal, see? That's my proposition,
ye can take it or leave it but. The position
is simple, you want a hoose, I say
for eight hundred pound it's yours.' And they,
trailing five bairns, accepted his omission
of the foul crumbling stairwell, windows wired
not glazed, the damp from the canal, the cooker
without pipes, packs of rats that never tired—
any more than the vandals bored with snooker
who stripped the neighbouring houses, howled, and fired
their aerosols—of squeaking 'Filthy lucre!'

Edwin Morgan

Visiting Belfast

1947

The Lisburn Road. As a boy
I served in the 'General Stores'
Scooping sugar from a sack
That stood unyielding
And solid as a bomb.

The cheese-cutter's handles
Were shaped for gripping.
Arms quivered as I pulled hard down
On the wire until cheese lay
Sliced on the marble slab.

With knife held low I would
Sneak behind the counter
And stab my uncle in the back.
The blade recoiled on its spring.
King Billy ruled the gable ends.

1977

Early morning at the docks
And there are soldiers
Who clearly mean business
But no taxis or buses
As a strike stuns the city.

Outside the dock gates
Men stand in doleful groups.
A soft mizzle drifts off the lough
Where gulls wheel, waiting.
The wharfs lie idle.

From his sandbagged roof
An observer scans the streets.
Derelict houses are shuttered
With corrugated iron.
Skag, and Billy, rule all the walls.

Wes Magee

The Inner Ring Road

Admittedly we didn't have to slave
Or give our feudal lord three days a week
To build this road, but paid our rates in lieu.
Walking along the monotonous pavement
I see my way too far ahead
And feel as small as I was meant to do;
Or I use a subway with fluorescent lighting
Broken and repaired and broken and repaired and broken and
   repaired,
With one of the slogans answered in Urdu—
A paradise for muggers. Streetlights above
On skyhigh standards confiscate our shadows
And the pavements, I hear, are regularly watered
With herbicide to keep wild flowers out.
Here below the man-made cliffs of buildings
We exercise in our open prison yard.
The Inner Ring Road will one day make
A wonderful ruin.

Stanley Cook

City

What would my Grandma have said
If she could have seen the green
Where once the houses stood,
Last year with red-black brick
And rotten boards and broken glass?

Would she have loved new grass?
Or would she just have moaned
About the loss of foggy yesterday
Where she and Grandad used to play
With whips and spinning tops
Between old cobblestones and chased
Wild arrowed boys back home
Along the narrow alley ways?

John Kitching

Autumn in the Park

The sun which we at first
Had thought was lost in mist
Steamed through to clear the day.

And green and yellow, golden, brown,
The leaves furled idly down and down,
Twirled breezeless round and down
And down to meet the Autumn ground.

As we walked through the park
Just like the sun, not lost,
We saw what seemed a froth
Of ash at feet of trees

And ran to crunch the meal—
Dead leaves that soon would heal
The cruel heat of summer
And would greenly bring
In their good budding time
Another fresh and urgent spring.

John Kitching

Snack Bar

Non-stop at the counter corner
The wedge advertising Fresh Cool Milk
Revolved in its private dilemma.

Against the wall someone was fighting
The space invaders for all he was worth
While the rain outside bubbled in puddles.

Old men on buttered teacake who had given up
Even investing in the football pools
Rolled memories to each other between the cups.

Slack time, with room for shopping bags to sit,
As we sat at our glass-topped table
Waiting for more than the rain to stop.

Stanley Cook

January Sales

The night is cold, the city street
Rings or taps with urgent feet
Of men and women hurrying home.
In gutters, banked like solid foam,
The frozen snow is still heaped there.
The traffic groans in misty air.
The windows of the larger shops
Throw on the pavement yellow slops
Of brightness though the stores are closed.
In warmth, behind the glass, are posed
Slender ladies, exquisite
In furs or silks; they stand or sit
At perfect ease, with studied grace,
Disdainful looks on each wax face.
But on the pavement looking in,
One lonely woman, pale and thin,
Shabby coat and heavy shoes,
Stares as if about to choose
Which lovely creature to become

When miracle or lucky sum
In sudden envelope arrives,
The magic which makes ageing wives
Walk beautiful as fairy queens,
Forget the cold, the price of greens.
The envelope will never fall,
Yet magic of a kind exists
Here and now as, through the mists,
You see her face, no longer old,
Indifferent to the teeth of cold:
The dreaming look of one beguiled,
The rapt expression of a child.

Vernon Scannell

Cries of London

the busker and his echoes in the subway
    the fans wild-singing on the train
        the mugged girl weeping in the precinct
            the rain

the marchers and their banner-calls for justice
    the juke-box belting in the bars
        the old jane cursing in the washroom
            the cars

the taxis as they screech along the highway
    the bill-boards with their scarlet words
        the news-stands bold and brash with headlines
            the birds

the tube trains as they squeal into the station
    the crazed drunk yelling out his fears
        the hookers touting for the nude show
            the tears

the dancers as they fall out from the disco
    the weirdo beat up by the boys
        the wet streets filled with teeth and voices
            the noise

Wes Magee

Incident on the Housing Estate

Day long the street lamps diffuse orange light.
From one a bicycle tyre hangs. Mongrels,
Macho curs of the precinct, roam in packs.
Set deep among the regiments of homes
A corner shop stands adrift in litter,
Its flagstoned forecourt stained with spilled Cola,
The grass verges threadbare. Here two youths battle,
Vicious and blatant, scattering shoppers.

I stop the car and order them to part.
One flings a 'stuff off out of it', then fells
His opponent, slams knees on a thin chest.
Mucus swings from his nose like nylon string,
As he pummels the boy's face before they
Roll, rise, and run flailing amidst traffic.
They part, hurling abuse harsh as their fists.
Thunder raindrops of blood stipple the flags.

I drive away, shaken, seeing anew
This vast estate where I have worked for years;
The weary, pre-cast houses, gardens grey
And useless, the squads of shouting children.
A punctured space-hopper lies dead in a
Gutter. Crude sex is spelled out on the walls.
Evening hauls down steel shutters and street lamps
Droop with shame. That we have come to this, this.

Wes Magee

A Voice from the Inner City

I am sick of the killing.
Young boys' dreams stand still in their hearts.
I am sick of people
tearing hair out from everywhere;
but doing nothing!

Teachers set me up with, no-how.
I am wise and ready
to serve the recent army;
Brixton's heavy industry, liberty relief.

Ratta tat tat,
Ratta tat tat,
Boom boom boom!

The respectabghetto charlatan
in the service of the system,
claws his distinguishing satchel to his chest;
He shouts quietly,
'There are no jobs.'
He shouts loudly,
'My organization will defend your human rights!'

LIAR! PHILISTINE!
God, what will tomorrow bring?

I am sick of the killing
of the unborn future;
uptown in Bristol,
downtown in Liverpool.
Rubber bullets and the gas C.S.
keep the natives to their natural place;
and they keep the peace with truncheons.

I am sick to the gall of the killing,
the unnecessary loss and pain.
I fear the frightening roar of the times
and the horrifying tide rushing on.

I stand by the river,
Watching the waves surging wild,
A broken whip float swiftly out with the tide.
No sun to tell the time,
but time is running out
I know, time is definitely running out.

The anger I believe was dead
rise up in me again;
No job,
No money,
No food.

Time is definitely running out.

Rudolph Kizerman

CAUSE FOR CONCERN

What's in the paper?	Iain Crichton Smith	22
Summer Song	W. W. Watt	22
Separate 'Development'	Leo Aylen	23
The Irish Jokes	Wes Magee	24
Open Heart University	Spike Milligan	24
The Fish are All Sick	Anne Stevenson	25
In the New Landscape	Bruce Dawe	25
All Animals Are Equal	James Kirkup	26
The Last Tiger	Gareth Owen	28
Market Square	David Wevill	29
The Mother	Edwin Morgan	30
Murder	Edward Lowbury	31
Euthanasia	John Kitching	31
Euthanasia	Elizabeth Jennings	32
Old Age Report	Adrian Mitchell	33

What's in the Paper?

What's in the paper this morning?
I walk with my morning rolls
down beside the water
where the tide withdraws and fills,

and read about thefts and murders
armies with shining guns,
lovers who've lost their lovers,
space with its million suns,

car smashes, robbers of banks,
old women who've won the pools,
a lion that lives in a garden,
riots in African schools,

a chimpanzee who paints pictures
all by himself in a room,
astrologers plotting the future
whether of hope or of doom,

ads that tell us that beauty
can be bought in particular pills,
lovers by candlelight talking,
cars that turn on three wheels.

And the tide is withdrawing, returning,
as it's done for millions of years,
and the paper's white in the morning
with its cargo of laughter and tears.

Iain Crichton Smith

Summer Song

(After a surfeit of irresistible ads)

I have spot-resistant trousers,
And a crease-resistant coat,
And a wilt-resistant collar
At my thirst-resistant throat.

I've a shock-resistant wristwatch
And two leak-resistant pens,
And some sun-resistant goggles
With a glare-resistant lens.

I have scuff-resistant sneakers,
Over sweat-resistant hose,
Also run-resistant nose drops
For my pollinated nose,

And my stretch-resistant muscles
Groan in work-resistant pain
While my battered conscience tussles
With my thought-resistant brain.

W. W. Watt

Separate 'Development'

A boy and a girl out walking one evening
With the sun golden, the peaches ripe,
On the wall of the old fort stopped to listen.
His face glittered in a ray of light.

He laughed as he dropped his hand on her shoulder.
Her face in shadow looked up at his.
Their friend, delighted by the warmth of their loving,
Took a photo of the moment they moved to kiss.

The picture won awards, was in exhibitions,
Was published more than once in glossy magazines.
But to everyone's astonishment was then impounded
As politically subversive, dangerous and obscene.

For although the lovers were Broederbond children
And upheld the government whenever it was attacked,
Silhouetted in the photo the girl looked Coloured—
An offence against the Immorality Act.

Leo Aylen

The Irish Jokes

They spread alarmingly, ethnic caricatures
Featuring Irishmen as thick Micks with huge hands.
They are the club comic's cheap laugh, swelling his sad
Repertoire of in-law, wife, Jew, and blue funnies.
Daily they creep up and jab your shoulder, as now:
How can you spot an Irishman in the car wash?
          He's the one on the bicycle!
Germ-like they pass from mouth to mouth, a verbal 'flu
Which children quickly catch and bring home loud from school.

Perhaps it's the notion of being green as a Treen
Or living on a leaky raft in the Atlantic
Or sheer despair at the chain-reaction killings:
Humour as rank as marsh-gas when all solutions
Founder against nailed sheets of corrugated iron.
One can but listen and smile as the jokes hit home,
          Bullets of fun leaving you weak
At the knee-caps. They will continue to trouble,
Like laughter heard in bars where bombs burst just last year.

Wes Magee

Open Heart University

Dedicated to BBC-TV Open University

We've come a long way
        said the Cigarette Scientist
as he destroyed a live rabbit
            to show the students how it worked.

He took its heart out
            plugged it into an electric pump
            that kept it beating for nearly two hours.

I know rabbits who can keep their hearts
                beating for nearly seven years.

And look at the electricity they save.

Spike Milligan

The Fish are All Sick

The fish are all sick, the great whales dead,
The villages stranded in stone on the coast,
Ornamental, like pearls on the fringe of a coat.
Sea men, who knew what the ocean did,
Turned their low houses away from the surf.
But new men who come to be rural and safe
Add big glass views and begonia beds.
Water keeps to itself.
White lip after lip
Curls to a close on the littered beach.
Something is sicker and blacker than fish.
And closing its grip, and closing its grip.

Anne Stevenson

In the New Landscape

In the new landscape there will be only cars
and drivers of cars and signs saying
FREE SWAP CARDS HERE
and exhaust-fumes drifting over the countryside
and sounds of acceleration instead of birdsong

In the new landscape there will be no more streets
begging for hopscotch squares, only roads
the full width between buildings and a packed mob
of hoods surging between stop-lights
—so dense a sheep-dog with asbestos pads
could safely trot across
(Streets will be underground and pedestrians pale.
Motorists on the other hand will be tanned.)

In the new landscape there will be no trees
unless as exotica for parking-lots
—and weeds,
weeds, too, will be no more
And we will construct in keeping with these times
a concrete god with streamlined attributes
not likely to go soft at the sight or sound of
little children under the front wheels
or lovers who have wilfully forgotten
to keep their eyes on the road,
while by a ceremonial honking of motor-horns
we'll raise a daily anthem of praise
to him in whose stone lap are laid
the morning sacrifices, freshly-garlanded, death's rictus carved
on each face with the sharp obsidian blade
of fortuitousness (steam-hoses will be used
to cleanse the altar . . .)

And in the new landscape after a century or so
of costly research it will be found
that even the irreplaceable parts
will be replaceable, after which
there will be only cars.

Bruce Dawe

All Animals Are Equal

Zoos are concentration camps for animals.
The lords of creation
are imprisoned in them
by men who perhaps mean well
but who are really no better than
grinning tormentors.

In every zoo I visit, I can sense
the heartbreak and the boredom
of beasts who should be free.

And my own heart breaks, too,
when I watch the hyena
still, after many years of useless anguish,
trying to scratch his way out—
when I see the mad stare
on the faces of neurotic tigers,
the hopeless lethargy of lions,
the misery of monkeys,
the insane gabble of tropical birds
who cannot bring the sky inside their cages
and sing with grief
at their separation from the humble sparrows—
humble, but free.

They all preserve a natural animal dignity:
even in despair, dejection, loneliness and sorrow,
they show nobility far above ours—
for we, too, who go to watch our dumb friends
are their tormentors—and we can laugh
in safety, being free (or so we think) . . .
The mighty black gorilla
sits with his back to us—so rude!—
the seals refuse to play for us,
the panda chews insipid bamboos
and cannot be persuaded to have an adorable baby,
the polar bears beg for buns, but
with one massive paw ready to swipe . . .

The zoo officials excuse all this dementia
by claiming that zoos protect endangered species.
Well, the preservation of the gnu or the crested ibis
is not as important as the loss of one guinea-pig's liberty
and cannot be justified by
the slow extinction of a million other creatures
deprived of native jungle, savannah, forest, desert, veldt,
and whose sad souls languish night and day
in the animal concentration camps
of Tokyo, New York, Peking, Berlin, Vincennes, Regent's Park—
Auschwitz, Dachau, Buchenwald, Treblinka, Mauthausen,
   Theresienstadt . . .

James Kirkup

The Last Tiger

Soon there will be no more of us;
I am the last of all my tribe.
Here I wait Oh my father and mother
My fangs rotted to stumps and black blood
Amongst the clapboard hovels of the suburbs.
Here I wait Oh my sons who never were,
In the days of my dying,
The gun shot festering in my hollow side,
Filling my belly on the wind.
Here I wait Oh my ancestors
Amongst the tin cans and the dustbins
Gnawing at my broken paw,
The mighty kingdom of my spirit
Shrunk to a white hot tip of hate.
Here I wait Oh my cousins
To kill this old woman
Who will limp across the cinders
With two buckets in her hands.

But I have a dream Oh my gods,
I have a dream
That in my ancient burning strength
I will roam the cities of mankind
And screaming claw the stolen coats
Of you my honoured sisters and my brothers
From the backs of rich and beauteous ladies;
Thus, do not ask me why I hate women.

Gareth Owen

Market Square

In the store window
behind yellow glass
two .38's, two .45's
      (one with a hand-stitched holster)
a blackjack, a row of flick-knives

all cheap at the price

ammunition boxed among
the dead wasps and flies
gunmetal, nickel plate
wood rubbed smooth and eaten into by sweat

such as shines
on the passing, reflected faces
who pause here . . .
           And pause
at the store's other half

where behind the yellowing glass
the brothers Kennedy and Martin Luther King
stare beyond their portraits
blindly into the sun

their eyes not meeting the eyes

and an Easter message scrawled
in the same hand
that fixed the price on the guns—

'Brothers, remember and pray'
                  David Wevill

The Mother

I've no idea who the father is.
I took a summer job in a hotel
in the Highlands, there was a party, I
got drunk, it must have happened then
but I remember nothing. When I knew
I was pregnant I was almost crazy,
it seemed the end of everything.
My father—it was just impossible,
you have no idea what he is like,
he would certainly have turned me out
and made my mother's life unbearable
if it wasn't unbearable before.
If I can describe him, he is a man
who equates permissive with diabolical.
Reading about a drug-raid once at breakfast
he threw a chair across the room
and swore till he was purple—swearing's
all right, and malt whisky, and chair-breaking,
but not sex. I have sometimes wondered
how he got over conceiving me,
or perhaps—if he ever did get over it.
—I am sorry, this is irrelevant.
I wanted to say that I—that my actions
are not very good and I don't defend them,
but I could not have the baby,
I just could not, you do see?
And now I never want to have one,
that's what it's done to me. I'm sick
of thinking, regretting, wishing, blaming.
I've gone so dead I see it all
like pulled from someone else's womb
and I can almost pity her
till I remember I'd be best
to forget the loss was mine.

Edwin Morgan

Murder

Her labours at an end, she barely heard
  'Your baby was born dead . . . but deformed';
    The doctor's words. Said nothing. Perhaps thought,
Through tears, 'God's mercy! Think what I've been spared'.

But he had lied; his message should have been
  'Your baby is deformed; he need not live',
    And she would have cried, madly, 'Spare the child!
Letting him die would be a deadly sin'.

                        Edward Lowbury

Euthanasia

      My mongol child, why should you live?
      Just what of worth have you to give?
      What increase will the song you sing
      Bring to the national growth?
      Another mouth to feed at great expense,
      What's the sense of saving you
      Your twenty, thirty thoughtless years
      Which just mean tears for those
      Who have the wear and tear of care
      For all your lolling, clumsy days
      Which could be quickly closed
      At cheaper ease?

              Or so some say.
    'Which some?' perhaps we ought to ask.
    Do 'they' include the some
    Who do not know your gift
    For smile and touch and love
    And, most of all, your living gift
    That helps the meanest, giving, live.

                        John Kitching

Euthanasia

The law's been passed and I am lying low
Hoping to hide from those who think they are
Kindly, compassionate. My step is slow.
I hurry. Will the executioner
Be watching how I go?

Others about me clearly feel the same.
The deafest one pretends that she can hear.
The blindest hides her white stick while the lame
Attempt to stride. Life has become so dear.
Last time the doctor came,

All who could speak said they felt very well.
Did we imagine he was watching with
A new deep scrutiny? We could not tell.
Each minute now we think the stranger Death
Will take us from each cell

For that is what our little rooms now seem
To be. We are prepared to bear much pain,
Terror attacks us wakeful, every dream
Is now a nightmare. Doctor's due again.
We hold on to the gleam

Of sight, a word to hear. We act, we act,
And doing so we wear our weak selves out.
We said 'We want to die' once when we lacked
The chance of it. We wait in fear and doubt.
O life, you are so packed

With possibility. Old age seems good.
The ache, the anguish—we could bear them we
Declare. The ones who pray plead with their God
To turn the murdering ministers away,
But they come softly shod.

Elizabeth Jennings

Old Age Report

When a man's too ill or old to work
We punish him.
Half his income is taken away
Or all of it vanishes and he gets pocket-money.

We should reward these tough old humans for surviving,
Not with a manager's soggy handshake
Or a medal shaped like an alarm clock—
No, make them a bit rich,
Give the freedom they always heard about
When the bloody chips were down
And the blitz or the desert
Swallowed their friends.

Retire, retire into a fungus basement
Where nothing moves except the draught
And the light and dark grey figures
Doubling their money on the screen;
Where the cabbages taste like the mummy's hand
And the meat tastes of feet;
Where there is nothing to say except:
'Remember?' or 'Your turn to dust the cat.'

To hell with retiring. Let them advance.
Give them the money they've always earned
Or more—and let them choose.
If Mr Burley wants to be a miser,
Great, let the moneybags sway and clink for him,
Pay him a pillowful of best doubloons.
So Mrs Wells has always longed to travel?
Print her a season ticket to the universe,
Let her slum-white skin
Be tanned by a dozen different planets.
We could wipe away some of their worry,
Some of their pain—what I mean
Is so bloody simple:
The old people are being robbed
And punished and we ought
To be letting them out of their cages
Into green spaces of enchanting light.

Adrian Mitchell

CRIME AND PUNISHMENT

Jailbird	Vernon Scannell	36
I'm no good, that's what I've been told	Roger McGough	36
Harrassment	Frederick Williams	37
The Tidy Burglar	Leo Aylen	38
Parents	Julius Lester	39
The Man Inside: Poems by prisoners		
Here I am, sewing...	Peter D.	40
It's humans that they put in prison	Eddie S.	41
I wanted to send you roses	Paul M.	41
Do you know why you are doing it?	Alan K.	42
The Other Time	Peter Appleton	43
What's the Difference?	Laurence Lerner	44

Jailbird

His plumage is dun,
Talons long but blunt.
His appetite is indiscriminate.
He has no mate and sleeps alone
In a high nest built of bricks and steel.
He sings at night
A long song, sad and silent.
He cannot fly.

Vernon Scannell

I'm no good, that's what I've been told

I'm no good, that's what I've been told
ever since I remember. So
I try to live up to my reputation.
Or down to it. Thievin' mainly.
And drugs. You get used to prison.
Don't like it though, bein' cooped up.
That's why I couldn't work in a shop
or factory. Drive me crazy.
Can't settle down. 21 years old
and I look 40. It's the drugs.
I'll OD probably. Couldn't care less.
Rather die young than grown old.
I'm no good, that's what I've been told.

Roger McGough

Harassment

One evenin, me a com from wok,
An a run fe ketch de bus,
Two police start fe run me dung,
Jus fe show how me no hav no luck,
Dem ketch me and start to mek a fus
Sa, a long time dem a watch how me
A heng, heng, round de shop

Me say What? Heng round shop?
From morning me daa wok,
Me only jus stop,
And if onoo tink a lie me a tell,
Gwaan go ask de Manager.

Dem insisted I was a potential thief,
And teck me to de station,
Anyway, dem send and call me relations,
Wen dem com it was a big relief,
Fe se som one me own colour,
At least, who would talk and laugh wid me,

An me still lock up ina Jail,
So till me people dem insist that
Dem go a me wok to get som proof,
The police man dem nearly hit the roof,
Because dem feel dem was so sure,
That is me dem did have dem eyes on
Boy, I don't know what's rong
With these babylon men,
But dem can't tell one black man,
From de other one,

Anyway, when me reach me wok place,
Straight away de manager recognize me face,
And we go check me card,
Fe se sa me dis clock out

So me gather strength and say to de coppers,
Leggo me, onoo don't know wey onoo on about,
You want fe se dem face sa dem a apologize,
But wen me look pon how me nearly face disgrace,
It mek me want fe kus and fight,

But wey de need, in a babylon sight,
If yu right yu rong,
And wen yu rong you double rong,

So me a beg onoo, teck heed
Always have a good alibi,
Because even though yu innocent
Someone always a try
Fe mek yu bid freedom goodbye.

Frederick Williams

The Tidy Burglar

The burglar tip-toed across the lawn
That was cut like a carpet, sprinkler-smooth,
Past ornamental waterfall
And pale blue utterly algae-free pool,

Crossed the patio, brushed through vines
Dripping with bunches of ripe, black grapes,
Cracked a window, stepped inside,
Admired the decanters, the velvet drapes,

Examined the stereo, touched the pictures,
Feeling the texture of the jagged oil-paint,
Opened a cabinet with Georgian silver
And Tudor miniatures in intricate frames,

But took nothing. He went upstairs
To the master-bedroom's jewellery cases:—
A diamond collar, six rings, a rare
Black pearl, some rubies, a dozen bracelets.

His eye strayed to the rumpled bed.
Untidiness always drove him frantic.
He made it neatly, stacked cushions at the head,
Then, hearing a noise, left empty-handed.

Leo Aylen

Parents

Linda failed to return home from a dance Friday night.
On Saturday
she admitted she had spent the night
with an Air Force lieutenant.

The Aults decided on a punishment
that would 'wake Linda up'.
They ordered her
to shoot the dog
she had owned about two years.

On Sunday,
the Aults and
Linda
took the dog into the desert
near their home.
They
had the girl
dig a shallow grave.
Then
Mrs Ault
grasped the dog between her hands and
Mr Ault
gave
his daughter
a .22 caliber pistol
and told her
to shoot the dog.

Instead,
the girl
put the pistol
to her right temple
and shot herself.

The police said
there were no charges
that could be filed
against the parents
except possibly

cruelty
to
animals.

Julius Lester

The Man Inside: Poems by Prisoners

Here I am, sewing . . .

Here I am, sewing . . .
A stitch in time?
No, it isn't going to stop me
Having to sew the other
Nine million ninety-nine thousand
Nine hundred and ninety-nine.

Peter D. (28)
Offence: larceny
Sentence: 3 years

It's humans that they put in prison

It's humans that they put in prison.
It's humans that puts humans in prison.
It's humans that puts humans in prison because
They say they're not humans they're animals.
But I don't know any animals that puts animals in prison.

Eddie S. (47)
Offence: indecent assault
Sentence: 8 years

I wanted to send you roses

I wanted to send you roses—
   only they don't sell flowers here
   but they said I could have some free thorns.

I wanted to send you a bracelet—
   only they don't sell jewellery here
   but they said I could have some spare chains.

I wanted to send you a wrist-watch—
   only they don't sell time-pieces here
   but they said I could give you some empty hours.

I wanted to send you a dress—
   only they don't sell clothing here
   but they said I could give you a repaired mail-bag.

I wanted to give you a kiss—
   and they were very helpful about that.
   They said there was a fellow going out next week
   and he'd give it you if I gave him your name and
   address.

Paul M. (28)
Offence: grievous bodily harm
Sentence: 6 years

Do you know why you are doing it?

Do you know why you are doing it? You would say
You are doing it sadly out of regrettable necessity
And because you are unable to think of any alternative.
Perhaps in a moment of honesty you would admit too
That you are doing it in retaliation for the harm
And the anger we have caused you and your society.

Do you know what it is you are doing though?
Do you want to know or would you sooner not?
If you don't want to know though this still
Won't alter what are you are doing knowing or
   unknowing.

If you like to put it so we have demeaned others and
Therefore you are demeaning us. But you cannot
Separate us humans we are all indivisible and
Some of what you do to us you do to yourself.
You are not cleansing us, purging us, reforming us.
The anger and punishment you pour on us only
Generates retaliatory anger in us towards you
And the desire to get our own back. After all
We are not noble characters as you would be first to agree.
We do not ask for pity, sympathy, even forgiveness,
All we ask is that you think about what you are doing
And if you are satisfied go on but if you are not
Then stop. We cannot get out from the horizon-concealing
Walls you have confined us in. But you are freer
To consider in your situation such things as whether
Perhaps you too are also in a prison but a mental one.
Yes you put our bodies here for a sentence but our
Minds can and still do occasionally escape and fly free.
Do yours? Or are you serving a life-sentence in the
Terrible state of not even knowing you're doing it?

Alan K. (29)
Offence: using a firearm.
Sentence: 10 years.

The Other Time

He killed a man
In a drunken brawl
They tried him, hanged him.
That was all.

But he left his wife
Nearly penniless
She was raven-haired,
She was glamorous,

She had swooned in court,
She had caused a stir.
And the editor of
The 'Sunday Blare',

Aware of his readers'
Appetite
And judging she should
Be worth a bit

Hired a snooper
Round to her house
With an offer she thought
Quite fabulous.

If she'd lend her picture,
Lend her name
To a story about
Her life with Him.

They'd write it up
From what she said
Did she understand?
She understood.

'I've never had much.
I've still less now,
I need the money.
The answer's 'no'.'

As he rose to go
He noticed a medal,
Mounted and framed,
Above the mantel.

And asked her about it
Where was it won?
When did he get it?
What had he done?

'Oh, that,' she said.
'They pinned that on
The other time
He killed a man.'

Peter Appleton

What's the Difference?

The world (one often hears)
Must be full of murderers.
Not all that many are caught;
There are plenty walking about.

Sometimes they pull it off
And lead a blameless life,
Good to the wives they wed
By bashing in someone's head.

So it's natural to wonder how
They differ from me or you.
Conscience? Consciences are
As calm as they appear.

I can make out in the sea
That washes my memory
Storms as sombre as ever
Darkened to wicked weather;

Hatred so great it might
Press my fingers as tight
On windpipe or on gun
As now around this pen.

If conscience is a sea
It answers from day to day
To what the weather is like.
The rest is only luck.

Did your girl say no
When the storm began to blow?
Was somebody passing when
You happened to raise the gun?

Weather's another name
For imagination;
And if yours is blustery
It imposes on the sea

Billows that rear up higher
Than intention, even desire;
Or a slow enormous swell
That is more than enough to kill.

Laurence Lerner

LOVE

Loving	James Berry	48
Love	Iain Crichton Smith	48
When I phoned	R. Kingsbury	49
In the Youth Club	Iain Crichton Smith	50
A Whisper I Shout With	James Berry	50
She Said	Liz Hutchins	51
December Love	David Sutton	53
Christmas Party	Wes Magee	54
First Ice	Andrey Voznesensky	55
Our Love Now	Martyn Lowery	56
It's Over	Joan Davidson	58

Loving

If loving is a river
embraced in the ground
and is the face of barefeet
kissing the ground as it goes
it is longing in movement

If loving is a rock
sitting in the earth
and is the deep root
of a tree stilled blissfully
it is steadiness

If loving is a pig
wallowing in soft wet earth
and is a woman's body
supine in sunlight wash
it is discovery

James Berry

Love

They always go on about Love
on the TV ads and films,
they show you those great big cars,
and beautiful rings and things,

and my Dad is reading the Record
and my Mum is mending socks
and she's always saying to Dad,
'Why do you never talk?'

and there's this beautiful girl
and this fellow in a caff
and they're drinking bottles of wine
and the two of them's having a laugh

and my Mum says to my Dad
'Why don't you never talk?'
and he carries on reading the Record
and sometimes he looks at the clock.

Iain Crichton Smith

When I phoned

When I asked you out the other day,
You said you'd love to have a meal with me,
So we decided to meet outside the station at five,
And there I stood waiting for you to arrive.

When I phoned, your mother said you'd gone to see a film,
And wouldn't be back till nine.
When I asked if I could phone again that night,
She replied that that would be just fine.

You should have said no, or made an excuse.
You could've said you had to wash your hair.
But you said you would come, and gave me a smile.
Now I know you were lying all the while.

When I phoned again at half past nine,
Your father told me
That you still weren't there.
When I asked him when you would
Be home, he laughed and said
He really didn't care.

So here I am, sitting on your fence,
Playing with your neighbour's ginger cat.
Your father's told me twice to leave his flowers alone,
Now I can see him picking up the phone.

I think he's phoning the police,
But I don't care
No, I'm not going away.
I'm dying to see your face
When you come home, And hear just what you have to say.

R. Kingsbury

In the Youth Club

It's like this, I want to talk to her and I can't.
She's sitting at the table drinking orangeade
and the lads are playing pool.

I think I'd like to speak to her but I can't.
Big Hughie would come over and make fun of me.
I'd like to clear the table so she'd see,
or get three bulls with the darts.
But she doesn't seem interested. What's she thinking about?

My name's Robert, I'd say, and what's yours?
I wouldn't say they call me Chicken.
How about the pictures, how about
the dance in the Gateway Saturday night?

But she's bound to have someone else, she's so pretty,
and she isn't at all interested,
she just sits there with her orangeade.
But I know she knows I am here.

Iain Crichton Smith

A Whisper I Shout With

Listen me and hear me
little bigeyed—beautiful—
bighearted—gentle—

I want you to rush
in a my hiding place
and I to rush in your one

I want you come in and out
more and more with me
and we settle a togetherness together

I want we pass every limit
and I see you there
and you see me too

I want we rock and roll
under each other's skin
and we stretch each other's bones

Little bigeyed—beautiful—
bighearted—gentle—
hear me and listen me

I want your hair a stifle me
in curls of whispers
shoeless hatless defenceless

I want you fill me up
with all the eye you got
with all your ambition

I want my emptiness
the vessel what poured for you
and my excitement your capture

James Berry

She Said

She said:—You were very nice, quiet and polite,
She said:—You were considerate, well brought up,
She said:—You were happy and kind,
She knows you live 200 miles away,
She just can't understand us.

She knows I don't see enough of you,
She certainly makes sure of that,
She said I think of you too much,
She just can't understand us.

She said phone calls were too frequent,
She said they must stop; then relented and
She said two calls a week was enough,
She said ten minutes is sufficient for any news you've got.
She listens in I know she does,
She just can't understand us.

She saw my exam results,
She said that was the limit,
She asked what was in your letters that made me so distant,
She reads them now—then gives them to me.
She said that was the only way to prevent it.
I said 'Prevent what?'
She said she didn't understand me.

She said my letters were to be approved at first,
She said she'd read then post them,
She said she would,
She said any arguments were in vain,
She said I was too young,
She said you'd get tired then what would I do—no qualifications no job,
She doesn't understand us.

She said she'd posted my letters,
She said you haven't written back,
You are getting them aren't you,
She said you would she said
She said—she lied.

She's hurting me,
She's hurting you and your family,
She said—she says—she has said,
She will say—she will say no longer!
She cried when I left!
I don't understand her.

Liz Hutchins

December Love

The first time they went out was in December,
The twenty-second. As he walked her home
The pavements were alive with frosty glitter,
And long clouds lay milk-white beneath the moon.
He was too shy with wonderment to think
Of anything to say to her, and she
Said nothing either; only their two hands
Maintained a gloveless contact in the cold.
Frost or this nearness made his whole frame tingle.
He wondered: should he ask her for a kiss,
But did no more than wonder, something held him
Spellbound and all of his desire seemed powerless
Against this sudden holiness of love.
Once on the way they passed some carol-singers,
Standing with lanterns underneath a porch,
And stopped to listen. 'Silent Night,' she said.
'I love that.' 'Yes.' Now they were nearly home,
And on the corner of her road, where lamplight
Made sudden summer underneath the trees,
He stopped. She looked at him. He could not speak,
Only, taking her shoulders in his hands,
He kissed her awkwardly upon the cheek,
And then again, feeling her scented hair
Brush across his face, and through her coat
Her body trembling, whether for the cold
Or something else he could not tell. 'Tomorrow.'
'Yes,' she said, and that was all. They parted.

He walked home slowly underneath the stars,
And coming down the long hill from her home
Felt as if he could step off the earth
And walk instead the starlit avenue
That opened up between the drifting clouds.
Dreaming so, he came to the canal
And leaning on the parapet looked down,
Seeing the trembling stars suspended there.
The carol-singers could be heard far off
Proclaiming in the strange and holy night

The birth of love. He wondered what it meant.
Black as ebony and bright with stars,
The waters flowed beneath without a stir.
The church clock in the village struck the hour.

David Sutton

Christmas Party

The gifts are unwrapped,
Wine bottles emptied.
Darkness, a late guest,
Snuffs out room candles.
Time for night games; the
House a thrill of dares.

A built-in wardrobe
Is hide-hole for two;
There they make a nest
From shirts, winter coats.
Friends seek them out; shrill
Voices on the stairs.

Oblivious, they
Unwrap each other,
Share secret delights
And, later, leave the
House while revellers at
Windows watch them go.

The night is alive
With white butterflies.
Our Christmas lovers,
Radiant and warm,
Walk hand in bare hand
Through the falling snow.

Wes Magee

First Ice

A girl freezes in a telephone booth.
In her draughty overcoat she hides
A face all smeared
In tears and lipstick.

She breathes on her thin palms.
Her fingers are icy. She wears earrings.

She'll have to go home alone, alone,
Along the icy street.

First ice. It is the first time.
The first ice of telephone phrases.

Frozen tears glitter on her cheeks—
The first ice of human hurt.

Andrey Voznesensky

Our Love Now

I said,
>observe how the wound heals in time,
>how the skin slowly knits
>and once more becomes whole.
>The cut will mend, and such
>is our relationship.

I said,
>observe the scab of the scald,
>the red burnt flesh is ugly,
>but it can be hidden.
>In time it will disappear,
>Such is our love, such is our love.

I said,
>remember how when you cut your hair,
>you feel different, and somehow incomplete.
>But the hair grows—before long
>it is always the same.
>Our beauty together is such.

I said,
>listen to how the raging storm
>damages the trees outside.
>The storm is frightening
>but it will soon be gone.
>People will forget it ever existed.
>The breach in us can be mended.

She said,
    Although the wound heals
    and appears cured, it is not the same.
    There is always a scar,
    a permanent reminder.
    Such is our love now.

She said,
    Although the burn will no longer sting
    and we'll almost forget that it's there
    the skin remains bleached
    and a numbness prevails.
    Such is our love now.

She said,
    After you've cut your hair,
    it grows again slowly. During that time
    changes must occur,
    the style will be different.
    Such is our love now.

She said,
    Although the storm is temporary
    and soon passes,
    it leaves damage in its wake
    which can never be repaired.
    The tree is forever dead.
    Such is our love.

Martyn Lowery

It's Over

It began not long ago
and now it's over,

the fun and laughter,
the games and days
when the loving went
on and on,

the times and places
where we would meet,
the days and days
of secrecy.

We touched and talked
and shared
new moments together.
Now it's over.

Tears in my heart,
you in my eyes,
I am lonely.

Sun shines,
bird sings,
I remember you.

You were my first
and only lover.

Joan Davidson

OTHER PEOPLE

Labelled	Roger McGough	60
A Black Man's Song	Jimi Rand	60
The Driving Instructor	Ted Walker	61
The Man in the Street	Alan Bold	62
Mum's The Word	Alan Bold	63
Edication	Rudolph Kizerman	64
The Useless Punk Rocker	Leo Aylen	66
Song: Mad Sam	Alan Bold	67
Nock Nock Oo Nock E Nock	Jimi Rand	68
Worldwide	Fazil Hüsnü Dağlarca	70
Where the Rainbow Ends	Richard Rive	70
Janos Kovacs and Wife	Michael Perneki	71

Labelled

I live in a body labelled 'handicapped'
Stunted legs and arms askew
I live in a body I wouldn't have chosen
But then few of us do.

People say I'm brave
As though bravery were a choice
I learned early not to scream
For mine is an unheard voice.

The world is competitive
And I'm ill-equipped to compete
But I'm no less of a person
Because I'm not complete.

I live in a body labelled 'second-rate'
Though I feel second to none
When Society knows the difference
Then my battle is won.

Roger McGough

A Black Man's Song

I looked in the mirror.
What did I see?
Not black not white,
but me, only me.
            Coal black face
            with big bright eyes
            and lily white teeth,
            that's lil old me.
Yes I looked in the mirror.
What did I see?
I saw a fella
who's dear to me.

        Short broad nose,
        full thick lips
        and black kinky hair;
        man that's me.
Oh I looked in the mirror.
What did I see?
I saw a fella
as cute as can be,
        that must be me.
If you look
in the mirror,
what will you see?
        You may see black,
        you may see white;
        but you won't see me,
        no siree not me.
                Jimi Rand

The Driving Instructor

Some sail oceans single-handed,
Some climb Everest and survive;
Some, like Arthur Ernest Hopkins,
Teach beginners how to drive.

Intrepid Arthur Ernest Hopkins
Eats no breakfast. Off he sets
With nothing to sustain him save
Adrenalin and cigarettes.

At nine o'clock Miss Ethel Clampett
(Eighty-two if she's a day)
Down some tranquil cul-de-sac
Has backed into a brewer's dray.

Ten o'clock: and Major Bullhorn
(In the War he drove a tank)
Executes a nifty U-turn
Through the wall of Barclay's Bank.

Neatly bandaged, at eleven
Hopkins takes the vicar's daughter
Three-point-turning near the lake;
Five-past finds them treading water.

At midday old Mrs Fidget
From Australia Avenue
Is making progress like a jumpy
Paranoiac kangaroo.

Arthur spends a thoughtful lunch-hour
Filling holes with fibre-glass
(Which yet might keep his skull intact
If nothing worse should come to pass.)

At two o'clock a teenage madman
Terrorises Tooley Street
Doing ninety in reverse
And signalling with both his feet.

At precisely three o'clock
Arthur's pupil gently backs
Between the level-crossing gates
And stalls the engine on the tracks.

At four o'clock there is no lesson.
Nor at five. At six, a jolly
Undertaker sticks an L-plate
On to Arthur's coffin trolley.

Ted Walker

The Man in the Street

He reads his daily newspaper:
Wars are breaking out everywhere.
He says he doesn't damned well care.

He fixes his eyes on a screen,
Watches murderous scene after murderous scene.
He never asks what that might mean.

Vaguely he believes there is a God.
He has enough to eat, a roof above his head.
His kids will be provided for when he is dead.

He has been born, has done a job, will shortly die.
He is respected and respects respectability.
He has served his time on earth.
                                        I wonder why?

Over his tombstone the gulls complain.
Grey clouds are lit by a glorious sun.
Like a rubber ball, the world bounces back without this man.

                                               Alan Bold

Mum's the Word

she has washed the dishes
done her hair
taken care of the cat
she has toddled with her
tribal load down to
    the laundromat

she has bought tokens
for the washing powder
paid three new pence
for bleach she has borrowed
a hardback thriller stuffed
her linens
    into the breech

she has sat for twenty minutes
as the wash flapped round like
flags caught in a rainstorm
or like soggy paper bags
sucked into a whirlpool

she has used the spin dryer
to wring shirts by the neck
and twist the guts from pillowslips
and remove every speck of
    messrs grit & grime

she is a good mother to her children
who are nowhere to be seen
who might be dying on the roads
—but their knickers will be clean

Alan Bold

Edication

Hello operata,
Kin you get me Kingston Jamaica sah?
I wanta speak to mah boy Bobby,
de numba is
JA five zero zero five.
How yah mean wha' JA stan fuh?
Wha' wrong wid yo'
it stan fuh Kingston Jamaica man.

Berr berr, berr berr, br . . .
Dat you Bobby?
Whasa matta son, you alrite?
Dint I always tell you
I gwine give you ah big surprise?
Well son, yo' lucky day come at las'.
Mek I tell you son,
yo' ole Ma win de London football . . . . .

What?

You mean you neva hear bout de football pools?

Oh,

well is dat I win.
How what?
De line bad man,
ah seh de line bad man!
Can' hear a ting ya seh.
Oh, how much!
Fifty thousand son,
fifty thousand pounds.
Ef I comin' home?
Ya mean to JA?
Wha' do ya boy,
of course I comin' home,
not before I buy you all what you need dough,
ah got you most everyting a'ready, from mail orda,
I even bought you a bran' new use' car.
Ah doan tink you preciate what I doin' for you Bobby,
doan tink you preciate it at all.

What you tryin' to seh?
Rupert Ma bought 'im what!
Bought 'im edication?
Is you gone crazy Bobby?
You doan have to worry bout Rupert,
yo' Ma got money now,
you jus' fine out where Rupert Ma got it
I will get it if you wants it son,
you doan have to explain anyting.

God, dis young generation got such funny tase,
I neva tase College in mah life;
how you cook it son,
wid rice?
I hear one of de woman at de People Social Club
braggin' bout er chil'ren goin' to Univercity,
Mussa some home in de country.

Hear one of dem:

'My girl Jermin goin' Oxford,
she gwine get good edication dere,
like de rich folks.
Wen she gets her scrolls I gwine put dem in frame'.

For dem boastin',
de Holy Saint done scratch dem off him book.
Talk talk talk all de time, bout wat dem chile do.

Wat ya mean I done undastan'?
Oh . . . . . ya seh college is ah school?
Course ah know dat.
But wait!
College really supply all dose tings you seh?
I is a real fool man;
Good ting you got booklearning son,
so w'en we is out in company, yo' ole Ma doan shame yo'.

Nex' club nite I gwine mek dem crazy,
specially w'en I tell dem you gwine to college too.
What ya say?
You wants to be a lawyer?
Bless yo' sweet little heart.
I gwine give you de bigges' sen-off
London town eva see.
I will get my bank to sen' yo' passage befo' de cock crow.
So I see ya w'en I see ya;
But rememba dis w'en ya come,
no blonds, jes' edication.

Rudolph Kizerman

The Useless Punk Rocker

'I'm gonna be a punk rock star.
I've devised a fabulous act:—
I drive on stage in a bashed-up car
Wiv me 'ead in a dirty sack.
Jump from the car, grabbing a chick
In one of the front few rows,
Rip off 'er dress and give 'er a kick
Right on the bridge of 'er nose.
Run through the audience, snatching bras
To pile on top of the speakers—
That'll send 'em into their oohs and ahs
And let loose the freaks and streakers.

I set the underclothes on fire.
The amplifiers catch
In a great blaze of electric wire
And shrieks like a football match.
Wiv the audience caterwauling in panic,
Birds setting light to their hair,
I sing the one song I can manage—
The Londonderry Air.'

Leo Aylen

Song: Mad Sam

There were few who walked past midnight
In the heyday of Mad Sam
When he stalked in his favourite jacket
Through the streets of Rottingham.
Yes, the bolts were snicked each evening
As the word went rumbling round
From tenement to tenement:
Mad Sam has gone to ground.

He'd been in and out of prison
Since he'd left school at thirteen
And made an early reputation
For being hard and fast and mean.
But as Sam became an older man
His legend lingered on
And he had to fight almost every night
Or see his reputation gone.

Now his limbs were getting slower
And his face was getting scarred
And it was frightening to keep being fearsome,
Harder to prove he was hard.
And a young man said: 'Sam, let's face it,
You're a hasbeen who's had his day,
So crawl back home to your little lady
And in future keep out of my way'.

Well Mad Sam's eyes were burning
And he lashed out with his feet
And the sounds of two men fighting
Went crashing through the street.
But the young man knew Sam's measure
And he stuck him with a blade,
Then walked upright through the darkness
And left Mad Sam for dead.

Now there are few who walk past midnight
Who remember old Mad Sam
Or remember his reputation
Now his fists and feet are gone.
Still the bolts are snicked each evening,
Someone else is number one.
So remember to hate your neighbour:
Do him or you'll get done.

Alan Bold

Nock Nock Oo Nock E Nock

Me was fas asleep in me bed
wen a nok come pun me door;
bright and early, fore day morning
before dawn bruk.
Nock nock—nock nock,
badoombadoom nock nock
badoomnock nock nock
badoombap nock badoom nock
who dat; a who dat nock?
E nock.
Is wha ya mean e nock?
You wha nock.
No, no, no e nock
You nock.
No no e nock,
E nock gwine sen ya back.
Back ta weh?
Back ta wha?
Back ta weh ya come from.

Why him gwine da dat?
Wha me da?
Ya na da natin, but him sey,
sen dem back,
sen dem darkies back,
sa ya hav a ga.
Wha me wan a no is,
'f me na da natin
why him sen me back?
Him sey ya too many
ya palute de place.
Me na palute natin.
Him sey ya na wok,
ya na tek ya opportunity.
Sa ya hav ta ga back,
ta little England.
To Trafalgar Square and Lord Horatio Nelson?
Back to *Bimsha*?
Weh de paople dem cook wid salt
and de food nice?
It nice nice ya no.
De breadfruit, cassava
sweet potato, pumpkin,
eddoes and yam
dem mek me mout water
and de sugar-cane,
wid de licker straight from de factory,
or de sea-egg and cat-fish and 'ting,
and don't talk 'bout de flying fish,
or de fruit tree.
Why me na see guava heh,
nor mammy apple, starch apple,
sour-sop, papau, golden apple
and all dem 'ting;
Coconut water and mount-gay rum.
Is he gwine sen me back ta all dat
eh eh! A mus ee really do like Bear Rabbit
is sa it ga? Me glad ya nock—e nock.

Jimi Rand

Worldwide

Here or in India or in Africa
All things resemble each other.
Here or in India or in Africa
We feel the same love for grains.
Before death we tremble together.

Whatever tongue he may speak,
His eyes will utter the meaning.
Whatever tongue he may speak,
I hear the same winds
That he is gleaning.

We humans have fallen apart.
Boundaries of land split our mirth.
We humans have fallen apart.
Yet birds are brothers in the sky,
And wolves on the earth.

Fazil Hüsnü Dağlarca

Where the Rainbow Ends

Where the rainbow ends
There's going to be a place, brother,
Where the world can sing all sorts of songs,
And we're going to sing together, brother,
You and I, though you're white and I'm not.
It's going to be a sad song, brother,
Because we don't know the tune,
And it's a difficult tune to learn.
But we can learn, brother, you and I.
There's no such tune as a black tune.
There's no such tune as a white tune.
There's only music, brother,
And it's music we're going to sing
Where the rainbow ends.

Richard Rive

Janos Kovacs and Wife

In his country they called him unemployed,
  in another, he was a tramp,
  in the next he was an 'undesirable element'.

He was expelled from one country
  because he worked without a labour permit,
  from the next,
  because he wouldn't work even with a labour permit,
  from the third: because he paid no taxes,
  from the fourth: his passport had expired.

In the fifth country he got married,
  his wife was deported from his side,
  while he was returned to his own country
  where he was jailed as an army deserter.

Taking up his bundle again,
  he landed in Number Three country.
  For years, he discovered, he had been wanted for tax-fraud,
  he was kicked out again and received the news
  that five years before he had sired a child.

With happy joy he rushed to find his wife,
  but he was caught on the way
  and jailed for illegal entry.

After a long while he got a letter,
  she wrote from over the seas,
  asking for his papers to arrange his visa.

He sent her the only one left
  which hadn't been lost in some office.

In the meantime the world went mad,
  even those who had a sackful of papers
  became suspect if they were alive,
  somehow he was taken for a Jew
  and shut up in a concentration camp.

There he was lost tracelessly.
Neither Reuters nor Havas has yet
reported to the world
what's happened
to Janos Kovacs, Hungarian worker and his wife,
nor to his small son born on the way.

Michael Perneki

WAR

Definition	Laurence Collinson	74
Bullets	Sipho Sepamla	74
Epitaph	Grigor Vitez	75
Notes for A Movie Script	Carl Holman	76
Kill the Children	James Simmons	76
No Surrender!	Wes Magee	77
Bomb	Timothy Palmer	78
There Was a Planet	faye hoban	79
'If You Envisage Nuclear War'	Gary Scott	80
No More Hiroshimas	James Kirkup	80
Open Day at Porton	Adrian Mitchell	81
The Choice	Robert Morgan	82

Definition

What is war my lord?
War is empire

What is war general?
War is manhood

What is war teacher?
War is inevitable

What is war preacher?
War is unfortunate

What is war fellow?
War is escape

What is war kind employer?
War is profit

Sister what is war?
War is a telegram

Brother what is war?
War is my impotency

Father what is war?
War is my trembling hands

Mother what is war?
War is three undiscovered graves

Laurence Collinson

Bullets

bullets
    are never nice things really
bullets
    are made to scare   to injure   to kill

bullets
        made by humans   are inhuman
bullets
        are cowardly persuaders   them vs hands
bullets
        brutalize the user   murderer by moral
                                              definition
bullets
        rip the flesh open   leave the heart inert
bullets
        pierced the backs of kids   killed and
                                          killed and killed

Sipho Sepamla

Epitaph

On the Soldier Fallen at the Time
of the Signing of the Armistice

The news flew swifter than the bird,
and swifter than the wind,
and swifter than the lightning.
The ether vibrated happiness.
But the news came late.

For those fallen it was much too late.

And had it come an hour earlier, he would now be alive,
shaking hands with comrades—laughing;
and had it come a day earlier, many more would be alive;
and had it come much earlier, still more would be alive.

They should have sent the message much, much earlier,
before there was the need of any dead.

Grigor Vitez

Notes for a Movie Script

Fade in the sound of summer music,
Picture a hand plunging through her hair,
Next his socked feet and her scuffed dance slippers
Close, as they kiss on the rug-stripped stair.

Catch now the taxi from the station,
Capture her shoulders' sudden sag;
Switch to him silent in the barracks
While the room roars at the corporal's gag.

Let the drums dwindle in the distance,
Pile the green sea above the land;
While she prepares a single breakfast,
Reading the V-Mail in her hand.

Ride a cold moonbeam to the pillbox,
Sidle the camera to his feet
Sprawled just outside in the gummy grasses,
Swollen like nightmare and not neat.

Now doorbell nudges the lazy morning:
She stills the sweeper for a while,
Twitches her dress, swings the screendoor open,
Cut—with no music—on her smile.

Carl Holman

Kill the Children

On Hallowe'en in Ship Street,
quite close to Benny's bar,
the children lit a bonfire
and the adults parked a car.

Sick minds sing sentimental songs
and speak in dreary prose
and make ingenious home-made bombs—
and this was one of those.

Some say it was the UVF
and some the IRA
blew up that pub on principle
and killed the kids at play.

They didn't mean the children,
it only was the blast;
we call it KILL THE CHILDREN DAY
in bitter old Belfast.

James Simmons

No Surrender!

This was the catch-phrase around Ulster's farms
when I was a boy. It came with a smile,
a certain nod of the head, a raised fist.
I saw it on crumbling walls in Belfast,
and read it in warehouses at the docks.
Back in Sheffield I repeated it like
a charm. Teachers told me to keep quiet.

My father was always ready with his
stories of Papes dumped in the village bog,
and I listened when he told how Fenians
crossed the border and rustled Armagh cows.
A cousin of mine stuck his head clean through
a window pane when he heard an Orange
flute band sashing its way up Duck Street.

Fenians, Orangemen, Black Saturday, Prods,
the Twelfth, no surrender. Names and phrases
I can roll around my tongue like pebbles.
Solzhenitsyn tells how Russian soldiers
were forbidden to surrender. Capture,
then release, meant imprisonment back in
the Motherland. Catch-22, plus some.

The Irish, the Russians; no surrender.
Half a world lies between Tyrone's green fields
and the wind ridden heights of Chelyabinsk,
yet the same phrase has been larynx tattooed.
It is croaked, a worry of syllables,
a constriction of sounds in thirsty throats.
In its noose men and women are throttled.

Wes Magee

Bomb

No, I don't seem to be very pre-
Occupied with the
Bomb, do
I?
It isn't that I don't care—after all, none
Of us want to be blasted to
Kingdom Come, do
We?—it's
Just that Gaye is prettier and a much nicer
Shape than a
Mushroom.
And then there's not much one
Person can
Do about it and there'll be all
Eternity to think about what we
Could have
Done.
Gaye. Isn't she
Sweet?
I'd go and call her now, but I've
Forgotten the
Number, and we're not on the
Phone and I'd
Probably be blasted to bits before I
Got to the
Call-box.

Timothy Palmer

There was a Planet

There was a planet long ago
Which once evolved a race
Of beings, noble, strong and wild,
Who moved with speed and grace.

The race 'matured', 'refined' and 'honed'.
Its people then broke free,
No longer needed nature's laws
The world was theirs, you see.

But sadly they could not foretell
The problems which would come:
When one tribe wanted dominance,
They built themselves a bomb.

Opposing tribes grew frightened then,
Afraid they'd pull the 'trigger'
'There's only one thing left to do',
They said, 'We'll build one bigger'.

A few objections faintly raised
Were lost among the noise
Of intellectual savages
Who played with nuclear toys.

We now look back on painted caves
On flint flakes in the ground
And wonder if ten years from now
We'll all still be around.

The relics of the past are there
To be observed by us.
Our relics may be nothing more
Than radioactive dust.

faye hoban

'If You Envisage Nuclear War'

Pour paraffin over yourself
Set fire to yourself
The result is the same.

Gary Scott

No More Hiroshimas

In the dying afternoon, I wander dying round the Park of Peace.
It is right, this squat, dead place, with its left-over air
Of an abandoned International Trade and Tourist Fair.
The stunted trees are wrapped in straw against the cold.
The gardeners are old, old women in blue bloomers, white aprons.
Survivors weeding the dead brown lawns around the Children's
    Monument.

A hideous pile, the Atomic Bomb Explosion Centre, freezing cold,
'Includes the Peace Tower, a museum containing
Atomic-melted slates and bricks, photos showing
What the Atomic Desert looked like, and other
Relics of the catastrophe.'

The other relics:
The ones that made me weep;
The bits of burnt clothing,
The stopped watches, the torn shirts.
The twisted buttons,
The stained and tattered vests and drawers,
The ripped kimonos and charred boots,
The white blouse polka-dotted with atomic rain, indelible,
The cotton summer pants the blasted boys crawled home in, to bleed
And slowly die.

Remember only these.
They are the memorials we need.

James Kirkup

Open Day at Porton

These bottles are being filled with madness,
A kind of liquid madness concentrate
Which can be drooled across the land
Leaving behind a shuddering human highway . . .

A welder trying to eat his arm.

Children pushing stale food into their eyes
To try to stop the chemical spectaculars
Pulsating inside their hardening skulls.

A health visitor throwing herself downstairs,
Climbing the stairs, throwing herself down again
Shouting: Take the nails out of my head.

There is no damage to property.

Now, nobody likes manufacturing madness,
But if we didn't make madness in bottles
We wouldn't know how to deal with bottled madness.

We don't know how to deal with bottled madness.

We all really hate manufacturing madness
But if we didn't make madness in bottles
We wouldn't know how to be sane.

Responsible madness experts assure us
Britain would never be the first
To uncork such a global brainquake.

But suppose some foreign nut sprayed Kent
With his insanity aerosol . . .
Well, there's only one answer to madness.

Adrian Mitchell

The Choice

They were landing and the great thrust
Pressed like magnetism on their bodies.
The great ship hovered then slowly
Dropped on meadow grass.

Starglyn, the captain, stared
At the green landscape.
Between two hills a deserted city,
Crumbling and overgrown, patterned
The Scanning Screen. The dials
On a Blue Screen indicated
No human life present.

Suncon, the Celestial Geologist,
Smiled over his captain's shoulder.

'You were right' said Starglyn.
'They must have been a very aggressive people.
What was your main source of information?'

'The great meteorite which broke
From Earth in 2048 A.D.
We took it to Station Z
And examined it. It told us everything.'

'What?' asked Starglyn.

'They were allowed to choose
Between good and evil.
And they chose evil . . .'

'Bloody fools' muttered Starglyn.

Robert Morgan

THE WORLD OF WORK

School Taught Me Leon Rosselson 84
Interview Iain Crichton Smith 84
Time to Work Alan Sillitoe 85
Reverie for a Secretary Stella Coulson 87
A Working Mum Sally Flood 88
A Bad Mistake Gregory Harrison 90
The Presentation Ripyard Cuddling 91
My Dad Iain Crichton Smith 92
Unemployable Gareth Owen 92
Redundant Alf Money 92

School Taught Me

School taught me
to write my name
to recite the answers
to feel ashamed
to stand in corners
to wait in line
to kiss the rod
to be on time
and trust in God
To make me a model citizen
That was their goal
Well I don't know about that
But it was useful training
For a career on the dole.

Leon Rosselson

Interview

When I went for this interview
this fellow sat at a desk.
'Hm,' he kept on saying
and then he'd stroke his moustache.
'Two O Levels,' he said.
'is that all you could manage,
after four years,' he said.
''Fraid that's all,' I said.
My Mum made me comb my hair.
'You dress up nice,' she said.
'Speak civil,' she said.
'Make sure you wear a tie.'
'Two O Levels,' he said.
'I'm afraid you really need
a little more than that.

For instance, say you had French.'
It was only selling hoovers,

going from door to door.

'Just an example,' he said.
It was raining hard outside
and my brown shoes got wet.

'And did you get the job?'
my Mum asked and then Dad
asked for his tie back.

I told her I didn't have French.

'You should have thought of that,' she said.
'Why didn't you think of that?'

Iain Crichton Smith

Time to Work

On looking in, it's hard to tell
whether Heaven is inside
or Hell.
Like all in life you're either sitting safe
with legs between the railings
or head stuck firm and wanting to get free:
if all that's good is good
three things to reckon with
are smell, and noise, and dazzle
beckoning from that machine-hall . . . . . .

Don't be shy: the sky's shut off
but lights light-up each *knight*
bent at a machine that runs
within its bulk instead of out.
Intensity is lavished on each steed
concrete-bolted to the floor
that works with arm-pulls
flash of spinning knuckles
creased brows, steady feet
and the calculating glint of eyes.

You'll soon be working one of those.
A pal already there three weeks
carries a medallion grin
as if three years press on his neck—
eyes asquint and fag in pocket
overalls with honourable map of oil
hands calloused, finger-stalled,
ears closed to noise that pushes
what is human to the walls.

Even Goldilocks looks in.
If all that's good is good
there's glory in machinery
and powder in the war-horse odours
reeking from the boards you'll walk on.
Tell me another, except
give us this day our daily sweat
that weekly pay will come.
The clock looks on, don't let it sleep,
make it follow limbs
you never knew you'd got,
wallowing in the drill and cut of work.

Neither Hell nor Heaven,
the only choice is walk in or fade out.
Machinery decides the spirit
that will break or stay:
Like the Twins in Heaven
both are born
on the same day.

Alan Sillitoe

Reverie for a Secretary

Feeling fragile and incredibly bored I listen to my boss
saying he takes five newspapers to get other viewpoints
from which he makes up his mind on world events.
I give him my look of awe thinking,
well bully for you, with a brain like that
you are paid nine times more than me?

Over his head and through the window
the sky is blue and beckoning. I wish I had wings.
'The return on capital investment is up two per cent'
Dear God, who really cares?
Wouldn't we be happier making daisy chains?
How disgustingly fat he is.
His hair parting would just fit an axe.
I am not brave. I can't walk out
leaving a question mark in the air.
I am your natural serving maid
dropping curtseys to the gentry.
Those figures are not correct?
How would you know?
You can only just crayon picture books.
He must know these figures came from the computer
and he supplied the original figures.
I could walk up and wack him over the head
with that dictaphone he can't use,
then drag him and push him out of the window.
From seventeen storeys he would splash.
Suicide while the balance of his pea brain was disturbed.
Mercy killer breaks down in dock.
Blond in penthouse drama.

He is looking at my legs and breathing through his nose.
Now he will ask about my boyfriend.
Here it comes right on cue.
'Yes, we went dancing last night.'
Stark naked and I gave myself to fifteen rugger players.
Should I tear off my clothes and scream rape?
They wouldn't believe me. They say he is one of those.
And now he wants a cup of coffee.
That's his seventh and he hasn't been to the loo.
My cool lily white hands deftly serve him
and my beautiful body glides round his desk.
My cool lily white hands want to pour it in his ear
and my beautiful body wants to dance as he screams.
He has hairs growing out of his nose.
I never noticed them before, and he reeks
of that lousy after shave lotion, yecch,
he doesn't even smell like a man.
Now he is going to lunch. Listen to him wheeze and puff.
'You will be back at three Mr Chatterton?'
Smile you bitch smile. He is bound to have a coronary
carrying all that blubber about.
Oh mummy, for this you made me do my homework?

Stella Coulson

A Working Mum

From morning, till night,
Life is one maddening rush.
The alarm bell rings,
You awake to a fuss.
Jump from your bed, to fight,
For a place on the bus.
Someone, who had stood
Close behind you
Now you discover
Is in front of the queue.

You don't want trouble,
So what do you do?
You stand there fuming,
The bus draws alongside,
A quick kick on her heel
Now you're climbing inside.
You smile at the conductor,
It's just made your day,
She's still looking around her
While the bus draws away.

You arrive in work
At the stroke of nine,
You clock your card
The weather is fine.
You smile all around,
'Good Morning' to you.
Then a voice in your ear
Bawls, 'Have you nothing to do?'
You sit down quickly,
You have laddered your tights.

Seems today you have
Nothing but frights.
You keep your head down,
You daren't look up.
The hooter blows,
You run for a cup.
The canteen is full,
Back in the queue.
You wait so long,
The hooter's just blew.

Though you feel thirsty
You have to get back,
If you dawdle too long
You will get the sack.
So you rush and you pant
Till you get through the day.
There goes the hooter,
You're now on your way.
You join the bus queue,
The one at the top.

The bus is full,
It won't even stop
You are hungry and cold,
You've had a long day.
No wonder your hair
Shows streaks of grey.
You have made it at last,
There is the gate.
Time for a cuppa?
'Mum, why are you late?'

Sally Flood

A Bad Mistake

'Stop the car,' cried the Boss,
'That man by the gate . . .
He's smoking and idle,
And certainly late . . .
I get rid of loafers . . .
How much does he earn?
Sixty pounds? He must think
I've got money to burn.
Well . . . there's a week's wages.
Pay him off. Make it clear
He'll not work an hour,
Or a minute more here.'

And the man raised his hand . . .
'O.K., Boss. As you like.'
And he picked up the notes
And rode off on his bike.

The Boss said to the gateman,
'What job did he do?'

'Oh, he ain't on the payroll;
He don't work for you.'

Gregory Harrison

The Presentation

After twenty five years they gave Geordie a watch;
Twenty five years in the same dreary notch.
They allowed him ten minutes to wash and to shine,
For to straighten his cap and get into line.

He stood in a row with another sixteen,
And they posed for a snap for the Work's magazine.
A company director presented the watch;
He shook Geordie's hand and he filled him a Scotch.

This important occasion had George in a flap
And he didn't quite know what to do with his cap.
He was out of his depth with these folk from the top
And he wished he was back at his bench in the shop.

Fine speeches were made by the cream of the firm
And the bouquets then handed made poor Geordie squirm.
There was one of the speakers, a man of great girth,
Who described men like George as 'The salt of the earth'.

There was patting of backs and they sang 'Auld Lang Syne';
There was plenty to eat and a surplus of wine.
They were toasted in whisky and showered with praise
And George and his pals spent the night in a daze.

But Geordie was glad when they called it a day
And when him and his mates had at last slipped away.
He loosened his tie, rubbed the sweat off his head,
Then he felt more himself, and his face was less red.

Then he looked at the watch which was clutched in his hand;
It was still in its box and it really looked grand.
He had bought it with sweat, but the price wasn't dear
For the cost to the firm had been ten bob a year.

Ripyard Cuddling

My Dad

'Walk tall,' said my Dad
'That's my advice to you'.
He worked for thirty years.
Now he's on the Bureau.

And he goes for a job and says 'Please'
And he slouches in a chair.
And he says to me 'Be sure
to cut that long hair.'

He used to walk tall, right enough,
and sing, 'I did it my way'
but now he gets up at twelve

Monday to Friday.

Iain Crichton Smith

Unemployable

'I usth thu workth in the thircusth,'
He said,
Between the intermittent showers that emerged from his mouth.
'Oh,' I said, 'what did you do?'
'I usth thu catcth bulleth in my theeth.'

Gareth Owen

Redundant

I was part of her once
yon Trawler, that stands in line
with the rest of her clan
that bob and sway
restless, all fast and tight
like shackled spectres

in the grey cold morning light
deck, galley, wheelhouse
and off shore breeze
are cluttered with older memories
rusting winches no longer turn
nor white foamed seas
surge bow or stern
or laden nets spew out
their silver harvest
from fathoms deep
all lie redundant now
in endless sleep
beyond the lock and gate
and wait, and wait
for oblivion
in the breaker's yard
while I
slowly, pass them by
and think of another
bleak tomorrow

Alf Money

REFLECTIONS

Back in the Playground Blues   Adrian Mitchell   96
Money   Carl Sandburg   97
Fantasy of an African Boy   James Berry   97
Life Insurance   Edward Lowbury   98
The Unbeliever   Edward Lowbury   99
Zen Legend   James Kirkup   100
The Not-So-Good Earth   Bruce Dawe   101
The Sensitive Philanthropist   D. J. Enright   101
Democracy   Langston Hughes   102
A Wish   Sipho Sepamla   103

Back in the Playground Blues

Dreamed I was in a school playground, I was about four feet high
Yes dreamed I was back in the playground and standing about four feet high
The playground was three miles long and the playground was five miles wide.

It was broken black tarmac with a high fence all around
Broken black dusty tarmac with a high fence running all around
And it had a special name to it, they called it The Killing Ground.

Got a mother and a father, they're a thousand years away
The Rulers of The Killing Ground are coming out to play
Everyone thinking: who they going to play with today?

> You get it for being Jewish
> Get it for being black
> Get it for being chicken
> Get it for fighting back
> You get it for being big and fat
> Get it for being small
> O those who get it get it and get it
> For any damn thing at all.

Sometimes they take a beetle, tear off its six legs one by one
Beetle on its black back rocking in the lunchtime sun
But a beetle can't beg for mercy, a beetle's not half the fun.

Heard a deep voice talking, it had that iceberg sound;
'It prepares them for Life'—but I have never found
Any place in my life that's worse than The Killing Ground.

Adrian Mitchell

Money

Money is power: so said one.
Money is a cushion: so said another.
Money is the root of evil: so said still another.
Money means freedom: so runs an old saying.

And money is all of these—and more.
Money pays for whatever you want—if
   you have the money.
Money buys food, clothes, houses, land, guns,
      jewels, men, women, time to be lazy
      and listen to music.
Money buys everything except love, personality,
      freedom, immortality, silence, peace.

Carl Sandburg

Fantasy of an African boy

Such a peculiar lot
we are, we people
without money, in daylong
yearlong sunlight, knowing
money is somewhere, somewhere.

Everybody says it's a big
bigger brain bother now,
money. Such millions and millions
of us don't manage at all
without it, like war going on.

And we can't eat it. Yet
without it our heads alone
stay big, as lots and lots do,
coming from nowhere joyful,
going nowhere happy.

We can't drink it up. Yet
without it we shrivel when small
and stop forever
where we stopped,
as lots and lots do.

We can't read money for books.
Yet without it we don't
read, don't write numbers,
don't open gates in other countries,
as lots and lots never do.

We can't use money to bandage
sores, can't pound it
to powder for sick eyes
and sick bellies. Yet without
it, flesh melts from our bones.

Such walled-round gentlemen
overseas minding money! Such
bigtime gentlemen, body guarded
because of too much respect
and too many wishes on them:

Too many wishes, everywhere,
wanting them to let go
magic of money, and let it fly
away, everywhere, day and night,
just like dropped leaves in wind!

James Berry

Life Insurance

A modest premium sets you free
From care: 'LET US INSURE YOUR LIFE',
Screams the blurb—a happy thought,
An instant immortality!

Who would not gladly pay much more
To be assured he will survive
Old age (the illness no-one dodges),
Or a thermonuclear war?

But look again: the Tree of Life
They show you has strange foliage;
Not leaves, but bank notes trained to drop,
Like fireballs, on your desolate wife.

Edward Lowbury

The Unbeliever

Do you expect me to believe
that a speck of earth divides
and multiplies and turns
into the double of God
by accident? that a chance
encounter of electrons
invented bone and muscle,
devised the lock and key of love,
instructed heart valves to steer
the blood, evolved the calculus?

and to under-write the dogma
that nothing need surprise me;
that beauty is voltage, discharged
by completion of a circuit;
that the Universe which used
to ring miraculous changes,
compelling adoration,
adds up to nothing more
than a computer programme?—
Well, I'm an unbeliever!

Edward Lowbury

Zen Legend

'Master, how may I find
the secret of life?'
—'Go into the remotest wilderness,
and when you have found it,
come and tell me.'

The disciple went into
the remotest wilderness.
For one year
he meditated.
But when he came to tell the Master
what he had found, the Master said:
'No, you have not found it.'

So the disciple went back into
the remotest wilderness.
For five years
he meditated.
But when he came to tell the Master
what he had found, the Master said:
'No, you have not found it.'

So the disciple went back again into
the remotest wilderness,
and without seeking for it
immediately found it.

But when he had found it
he did not come to tell the Master.

Then the Master
knew he had found it.

James Kirkup

The Not-So-Good Earth

For a while there we had 25-inch Chinese peasant families
famishing in comfort on the 25-inch screen
and even Uncle Billy whose eyesight's going fast
by hunching up real close to the convex glass
could just about make them out—the riot scene
in the capital city for example
he saw that better than anything, using the contrast knob
to bring them up dark—all those screaming faces
and bodies going under the horses' hooves—he did a terrific job
on that bit, not so successful though
on the quieter parts where they're just starving away
digging for roots in the not-so-good earth
cooking up a mess of old clay
and coming out with all those Confucian analects
to everybody's considerable satisfaction
(if I remember rightly Grandmother dies
with naturally a suspenseful break in the action
for a full symphony orchestra plug for Craven A
neat as a whistle probably damn glad
to be quit of the whole gang with their marvellous patience.)
We never did find out how it finished up . . . Dad
at this stage tripped over the main lead in the dark
hauling the whole set down smack on its inscrutable face,
wiping out in a blue flash and curlicue of smoke
600 million Chinese without a trace . . .

Bruce Dawe

The Sensitive Philanthropist

If I give you money,
Give you baksheesh,
Will you stay away
Until next week?

Since money talks
We don't need to,
Neither you to me
Nor me to you.

If I give you money
Will you make sure
That the others keep away,
Without me giving more?

Will you promise
To put to flight
All your legless colleagues
By day and by night?

If I give you money
Will you agree
To hide your stump away,
Where I can't see?

Will you state in writing
That it was done on purpose
And doesn't really hurt,
The arms, the legs, the nose?

Can't I send a cheque
Regular each week
By registered letter,
So we need never meet?

    D. J. Enright

Democracy

Democracy will not come
Today, this year
  Nor ever
Through compromise and fear.

I have as much right
As the other fellow has
    To stand
On my two feet
And own the land.

I tire of hearing people say,
Let things take their course.
Tomorrow is another day.
I do not need my freedom when I'm dead.
I cannot live on tomorrow's bread.

Freedom
Is a strong seed
Planted
In a great need.
I live here, too.
I want freedom
Just as you.

                Langston Hughes

A Wish

I have rivalled the birds in the air
enfolded by clouds even

I've been given to bend the sky at night

I am an atlas in my own right
holding back mighty rivers or changing their course

I defy distance reducing it to a point
as little as my hand

listen, I have pulled myself out of
the earth's warm womb glittering

I am that kind of man

but a wish of mine remains
peace at all times with all men

Sipho Sepamla

Notes

AM I O.K.?

Am I O.K.? (p. 2)
A poem about a feeling many people experience. The person in the poem feels insecure and seeks reassurance from the one person who can really give it.

I am (p. 2)
A fourth-year boy imagines himself as the different types of hero-figure he would like to be.

Disruptive Minority (p. 3)
A poem which first appeared as a poster poem in the Stepney area of London. Alan Gilbey expresses the frustration of a schoolboy who realises how limited his prospects are.

Westerns (p. 4)
The boy in the poem wishes he could stand up to another boy called Hughie, in the way that John Wayne, the actor who plays the good guy in the westerns he sees, stands up to Jack Palance, the actor who plays the bad guy.

Wen I Dance (p. 4)
James Berry expresses the joy and exhilaration a person feels whenever he dances.

Parent and Child (p. 6)
A young person expresses his determination to live his own life, rather than to allow his parents to dictate what he does, then reflects that he may not have any choice, since inherited characteristics may already dictate how he behaves.

Why? (p. 6)
A poem about someone for whom things never seem to work out. She wonders why.

As soon as I could speak (p. 7)
A poem which summarises the lives of many women. From *Bedwritten*, a collection of poems published by the Basement Writers.

Poem for my Sister (p. 7)
The high-heeled shoes are a symbol of the adult world. The older sister reflects how easily her sister moves about in her childhood world of games of peever (another name for hopscotch) and wishes she did not have to grow up to face the uncertainties of adolescence and adulthood.

I walked along some forgotten shore (p. 8)
An old man thinks about the person he has become and how the boy he used to be would not recognize him.

CITY SCENES

Streets of Childhood (p. 10)
Milly Harris writes about racial prejudice in London's East End. She refers to Oswald Mosley, leader of the British Nazi Party in the 1930s, and his followers,

the Blackshirts, so-called because of the black uniform they wore, and to the National Front, a political organisation, which spreads propaganda against communists, Jews and blacks.

The Mary Baker City Mix (p. 11)
Alex Glasgow expresses his feelings about modern cities and their lack of individuality. Mary Baker is a popular brand of instant cake mix.

Glasgow Sonnet (iii) (p. 12)
An unscrupulous property dealer sells two rooms in a slum apartment-house, already scheduled for demolition, to a homeless couple with five bairns (children). The poet's attitude to the deal is clear. 'Filthy lucre' means 'money made as a profit in a foul or filthy way'.

Visiting Belfast (p. 12)
Wes Magee contrasts scenes he recalls from his boyhood in Belfast in 1947, with the scenes he finds on a return visit to the city in 1977. The Lisburn Road is one of Belfast's main streets. The slogan 'Billy' refers to King Billy—King William III, a Protestant, whose success in seizing the throne from the Catholic James II owed much to the support of the Irish Protestants who helped his army to victory over James II's supporters at the Battle of the Boyne in 1690. The name 'Skag' appears all over the place in Belfast, on walls, corrugated iron barriers. It is someone's personal signature, like 'Kilroy was here'; an example of the incredible 'street writing and art of Belfast'.

The Inner Ring Road (p. 13)
Stanley Cook takes an appraising look at an inner ring road, describing some of its unattractive features and concluding that one day it will make 'a wonderful ruin'.

City (p. 14)
A poem about a slum clearance. John Kitching wonders what the old people, who lived and played there as children, would have felt about the change. Would they have welcomed it, or bemoaned it?

Autumn in the Park (p.14)
Walking through a park in autumn John Kitching reflects on the dead leaves he sees and how, in good time, another spring will follow.

Snack Bar (p. 15)
A poem about a snack bar at a slack time of day. The various descriptive details help us to visualise the scene. We can clearly picture the advertisement remorselessly revolving, the person at the space invaders, the old men swopping memories, the shoppers with their shopping bags on the empty seats and the rain pouring down outside.

January Sales (p. 15)
For those unable to afford luxury items, the January sales bring dreams of miraculous bargains, such as a fur coat or a silk dress. Vernon Scannell describes a shabbily-dressed woman gazing into a shop window and picturing herself wearing the clothes the models are wearing.

Cries of London (p. 16)
The selection of sounds described in this poem together create an impression of modern London, pulsing with violent life.

Incident on the Housing Estate   (p. 17)
A bleak poem. Wes Magee writes about an incident when he tried to stop two boys fighting. The incident causes him to distance himself for a moment from the estate where he works and to see it from a fresh viewpoint. The details he describes build up a depressing picture.

A voice from the Inner City   (p. 17)
Rudolph Kizerman protests at the deprivation in Britain's inner city areas. The references to Brixton, Bristol and Liverpool are to places where riots occurred in 1981. The 'respectabghetto charlatan' is a government official. A charlatan is someone who poses as a doctor. 'Respectabghetto' is a word coined from the words 'respectable' and 'ghetto', an area of a city where deprived people live. The term ghetto was first used to describe that area of a city where Jews were forced to live. The official is described as a Philistine, a term now used for anyone who is insensitive and uncaring. The Philistines were a warlike people who, in Old Testament times, harassed the Israelites.

CAUSE FOR CONCERN

What's in the paper?   (p. 22)
Iain Crichton Smith reflects on the contents of a morning newspaper. The poem leaves us to ponder the questions: 'What makes news?' and 'How important is the news we read in the newspaper and see on TV?'

Summer Song   (p. 22)
A humorous protest at the way our minds are bombarded with advertisements, making extravagant claims for products. A surfeit means an excessive amount.

Separate 'Development'   (p. 23)
A poem about the South African government's policy of apartheid, or racial separation—the 'separate development' referred to in the title. The Immorality Act forbids any sexual relationships between members of different racial groups. So the photograph of the couple was impounded (confiscated). The Broederbond is an Afrikaner society, or brotherhood, to which it is necessary to belong, if you are to rise to any position of authority, not only in the government, but even in a small town school.

The Irish Jokes   (p. 24)
Wes Magee writes about how Irish jokes reinforce prejudices by stereotyping Irishmen as 'thick Micks with huge hands'. He attempts to analyse why such stale humour continues to trouble him, the 'bullets of fun' leaving him 'weak at the knee-caps'—a reference to the I.R.A. punishment of crippling informers by shooting them in the knee-caps.

Open Heart University   (p. 24)
Experiments on live animals are permitted for the purposes of medical research. Spike Milligan voices his protest at an operation performed on a live rabbit, which was included in an Open University television programme, to show the students how the rabbit's heart worked.

The Fish are All Sick (p. 25)
Anne Stevenson issues a warning about what we are doing to the sea by not respecting it the way men used to do.

In the New Landscape (p. 25)
The Australian poet Bruce Dawe protests at the destruction of the environment, by portraying a future landscape in which there is nothing except for roads and cars.

All Animals Are Equal (p. 26)
James Kirkup questions the way we keep animals in zoos and asks whether even the claim that zoos protect endangered species can justify our doing so. He compares zoos to concentration camps and, in the last two lines, lists the names of some of the world's main zoos, followed by the names of some of the concentration camps that existed during the Second World War. The title of the poem comes from George Orwell's satirical novel, *Animal Farm*, in which the animals on a farm rebel and take control of the farm. They proclaim that All Animals Are Equal, but in the course of time the pigs seize power and the other animals are informed that while all animals are equal, some are more equal than others!

The Last Tiger (p. 28)
The hunting and killing of tigers for their skins has reduced the size of the world's tiger population to such an extent that the tiger could eventually become extinct. Gareth Owen imagines the thoughts which might be passing through the mind of 'the last tiger'.

Market Square (p. 29)
In the United States, it is possible for an adult to walk into a store and purchase a gun and ammunition over the counter. David Wevill writes about such a store. The reference to 'the brothers Kennedy and Martin Luther King' is to President John F. Kennedy, his brother Senator Robert Kennedy and the black religious leader, Martin Luther King, three prominent American political leaders, who were all shot and killed by assassins. David Wevill points out the irony that a shopowner who sells guns and ammunition should have a picture of three murdered men on display in his window.

The Mother (p. 30)
The young woman in the poem has just had an abortion. She explains her reasons for deciding to have an abortion and how she feels about it afterwards.

Murder (p. 31)
A poem about the right to life. In this case, the baby is physically deformed. The poem raises the questions: 'Should badly deformed babies be allowed to die?' and 'Who should make the decision—doctors, the babies' parents, society?'

Euthanasia (p. 31)
Euthanasia means mercy-killing. At present, euthanasia is illegal, but there are people who believe that a law should be passed by Parliament making euthanasia legal. Some people believe that euthanasia should be legal in the case of babies, such as mongols, who are born with severe mental handicaps. John Kitching outlines this argument, then reminds us that many mongols have very gentle, happy, affectionate natures.

Euthanasia (p. 32)
Elizabeth Jennings imagines that a law has been passed making euthanasia legal. She writes about it from the point of view of an old person.
Old Age Report (p. 33)
A forceful poem, which questions the way society treats old people, many of whom have to live out their retirement in poverty.

CRIME AND PUNISHMENT

Jailbird (p. 36)
A prisoner is often called a jailbird. Vernon Scannell's short poem draws out the comparison between a man in prison and a bird that the name suggests.
I'm no good, that's what I've been told (p. 36)
This is taken from a sequence of poems, *Unlucky For Some*, thirteen poems of thirteen lines, about people down on their luck. The boy in the poem has a very low self-image. Because he feels worthless, he has turned to thieving and then to drugs and at 21 he feels he has nothing left to live for.
Harassment (p. 37)
In recent times, the so-called 'Sus' law has caused much concern. Under this law, the police had the power to arrest anyone suspected of loitering with intent to commit an offence. The law has led to wrongful arrests and to conflicts between the police and many young people, especially young blacks. The black poet Frederick Williams describes the harassment of an innocent young black on his way home from work.
The Tidy Burglar (p. 38)
Not all burglars behave in the way that you might expect. Leo Aylen's poem is based on a true story, which happened in Los Angeles.
Parents (p. 39)
The chilling story of a terrible tragedy. Julius Lester's bald presentation of the facts without any comment emphasises the stark horror of what happened.
The Man Inside (p. 40)
These four poems were written by men serving prison sentences and are from *The Man Inside*, an anthology of writing and conversational comment by men in prison, edited by Tony Parker. The four men express their feelings about how inhuman prison life is. We are left to ask ourselves what is the point of sending people to prison, if this is how it makes them feel.
The Other Time (p. 43)
A poem about society's attitudes towards the taking of human life, written before the abolition of capital punishment in Britain. It asks: is it hypocrisy to have the death penalty for murder, while awarding medals to those who kill in wartime?
What's the Difference? (p. 44)
Laurence Lerner suggests that many murderers are no different from you or me, and that, at times, we too experience the feelings of murderous hatred that made them kill.

LOVE

Loving (p. 48)
A poem about what loving is. Each of the three verses suggests a different feature of loving—longing, steadiness and discovery.

Love (p. 48)
A teenager is reflecting on the nature of love. He contrasts the impression of love given by TV advertisements and films with the impression given to him by his parents' behaviour. *The Record*, which his father is reading, is a Scottish newspaper.

When I phoned (p. 49)
The boy in the song is let down badly, but is determined to confront the girl and not to let her get away with her inconsiderate behaviour.

In the Youth Club (p. 50)
A poem about a boy who lacks the confidence to go and speak to a girl he fancies. He senses she knows he is there, but can not fathom what she is thinking.

A Whisper I Shout With (p. 50)
A poem full of the excitement of being passionately in love. Almost breathlessly, the poet pours out what he hopes for from his newly-found love and how deeply he wants them to share their love.

She Said (p. 51)
A girl tells the story of her relationship with her boyfriend by repeating what her mother has said about it. We are not only given a clear picture of the mother's attitude to their relationship, but are also able to view the mother's baheaviour from the girl's standpoint.

December Love (p. 53)
Two young people discover their love for the first time one December evening. The magic of the moment is heightened by the fact that it is Christmastime, and the boy wonders what it all means.

Christmas Party (p. 54)
Two lovers find a place to be alone at a Christmas party. The other guests are forgotten as they share their love.

First Ice (p. 55)
For the first time, a girl experiences the pain of rejection and loneliness, when a relationship comes to an end.

Our Love Now (p. 56)
The contrast between what the man says, describing how things once were, and what the woman says, describing how things are now, shows how their relationship has changed.

It's over (p. 58)
Joan Davidson looks back wistfully at the good times she and her lover had together. The relationship is over, but the lover is not forgotten.

OTHER PEOPLE

Labelled (p. 60)
Roger McGough writes from the point of view of a handicapped person. The poem provides an insight into what it means to be labelled handicapped and what handicapped people feel about society's attitude towards them.

A Black Man's Song (p. 60)
A cheerful poem about a man's image of himself. Naturally, he sees all his features, not just the colour of his skin.

The Driving Instructor (p. 61)
A black comedy, in which an intrepid driving instructor survives a morning of misadventures, only to meet his doom in mid-afternoon, when a pupil stalls the car on a level-crossing.

The Man in the Street (p. 62)
A poem about the average man. Alan Bold reflects on his life and its significance.

Mum's the Word (p. 63)
This poem about a 'good mother' invites us to question the role played by this woman and many like her, and the attitude of children like hers, who take what she does for granted. In the title, the poet is playing with words. 'To keep mum' means to keep quiet, and the expression 'Mum's the word' means 'Keep it quiet'.

Edication (p. 64)
A humorous poem telling the story of a West Indian mother who has just won the football pools and is telephoning her son in Jamaica to tell him how she plans to spend the money. Her excited chatter gives us a clear picture of the type of person she is—someone who never had the chance to get the 'edication' her son wants her to buy him.

The Useless Punk Rocker (p. 66)
A poem poking fun at the lengths to which some performers are prepared to go in order to make their acts more exciting.

Song: Mad Sam (p. 67)
The story of a tearaway. Mad Sam represents all those people who seek to find an identity for themselves by fighting and building up a reputation for being 'hard and fast and mean'.

Nock Nock Oo Nock E Nock (p. 68)
Jimi Rand makes fun of the pressure put on British blacks by those who advocate what is euphemistically called 'voluntary repatriation', a policy of sending people back to the countries which their families originally came from. 'E nock', which literally means 'he knocks', is a play on words and refers to the British politician Enoch Powell, who has spoken out in favour of 'voluntary repatriation'. Bimsha is Barbados.

Worldwide (p. 70)
The Turkish poet Fazil Dağlarca writes about how the peoples of the world have lost touch with one another, allowing territorial barriers to come between them.

Where the Rainbow Ends (p. 70)
The South African poet Richard Rive dreams of a place—at the rainbow's end—where black and white people will one day live in harmony.
Janos Kovacs and Wife (p. 71)
This poem by the Hungarian poet Michael Perneki tells how a man and his family, during the 1930s, become victims of the economic and political circumstances of the time. Janos Kovacs's story reminds us of all those throughout the world who, at different times but for similar reasons, have suffered such a fate. Reuters News Agency, London and the Agence Havas, Paris were two of the largest international press agencies operating in the 1930s.

WAR

Definition (p. 74)
A poem which looks at war from a number of angles and reminds us that its legacy is suffering and grief.
Bullets (p. 74)
A poem from *The Soweto I Love* by the black South African poet Sipho Sepamla. This poem expresses the anger that was the natural reaction to the killings that occurred when police opened fire on rioters in Soweto, one of the black townships of Johannesburg, in June 1976.
Epitaph (p. 75)
An epitaph is a poem written on the occasion of someone's death, or an inscription written on a tomb. The Yugoslav poet Grigor Vitez writes an epitaph for a soldier killed at the time an armistice, or truce, is being signed, and remembers all those for whom the armistice came too late.
Notes for a Movie Script (p. 76)
Each verse is like a short piece of film. Carl Holman uses a series of images, each creating a different mood, to tell the story of a soldier and the woman who loves him. V-mail is the U.S. army mail.
Kill the Children (p. 76)
A poem about an incident in which some children at play were killed by a terrorist bomb in Belfast. The U.V.F. is the Ulster Volunteer Force, a Protestant extremist group. The I.R.A. is the Irish Republican Army.
No Surrender! (p. 77)
Wes Magee considers the implications of the term 'No surrender', the catchphrase of Protestant Loyalist groups in Ulster. Papes and Fenians are Catholics. Orangemen and Prods are Protestants. The Twelfth refers to the 12th of July, the day on which Irish Protestants celebrate the victory of William of Orange over the Catholic supporters of James II. Armagh and Tyrone are counties of Ulster. Black Saturday is an Orange day of celebration. Alexander Solzhenitsyn is a Russian dissident writer, now living in exile in the West. In his writings, he tells how when Russian soldiers, who were made prisoners of war during World War Two, returned to Stalinist Russia, they were immediately arrested

and put in labour camps. Chelyabinsk is a distant city in the depths of Russia, far away from Tyrone's 'green fields'. 'Catch 22' is a reference to the term 'A Catch 22 situation', a situation in which people are so ensnared by circumstances that whatever they do will not enable them to escape accusation, punishment or death. The term comes from the title of a novel, which describes people caught in such a situation.
Bomb (p. 78)
Timothy Palmer expresses the attitude of many people towards the bomb—'Of course I care, but there's nothing *I* can do about it.'
There Was a Planet (p. 79)
This poem, like the following one, comes from an anthology of writing and drawings, *Nuclear Fragments*, by people concerned about nuclear war and nuclear power. faye hoban reflects on where so-called 'development' has led us.
'If you Envisage Nuclear War' (p. 80)
Gary Scott presents a stark picture of what nuclear war would mean to an individual caught in an attack.
No More Hiroshimas (p. 80)
On 6 August 1945, a United States air force bomber dropped an atom bomb on the Japanese city of Hiroshima. James Kirkup describes a visit to the Park of Peace, a memorial in present-day Hiroshima.
Open day at Porton (p.81)
Porton Down is the government's top secret, biological warfare laboratory. Adrian Mitchell writes about a biological or chemical weapon and what its effect would be. The poem asks the question: can we justify the existence of such an establishment on the grounds that the only way to deter others from using such weapons is to develop them ourselves?
The Choice (p. 82)
A science fiction fable. Robert Morgan suggests that man's nature could lead him to destroy the planet on which he lives.

THE WORLD OF WORK

School Taught Me (p. 84)
Leon Rosselson suggests that, ironically, the kind of behaviour expected from you at school is a very good preparation for life on the dole. 'To kiss the rod' means to accept correction submissively.
Interview (p. 84)
A boy goes for an interview and fails to get a job. His mother's final remarks express their frustration that the interview proved fruitless.
Time to Work (p. 85)
Alan Sillitoe writes about the machine-hall that is to become a young man's workplace, now that he is old enough to start work.
Reverie for a Secretary (p. 87)
Stella Coulson reveals what a secretary really thinks of her boss, the job she has to do and the role she is expected to play.

A Working Mum (p. 88)
Sally Flood, a garment worker in London's East End, describes how life for a working mother is 'one maddening rush'.

A Bad Mistake (p. 90)
A cautionary tale with the message that it doesn't pay to act first, then ask questions afterwards.

The Presentation (p. 91)
Ripyard Cuddling is the pen-name of Jack Davitt, a welder in a Tyneside shipyard. He writes about the presentation of a watch to a man who has given a firm 25 years' service. He points out how hard the man had to work to earn the watch, but that it only cost the firm ten bob (ten shillings, or 50 new pence) a year.

My Dad (p. 92)
A young man reflects on how his dad has changed because he is now unemployed. 'On the Bureau' means signed on as unemployed.

Unemployable (p. 92)
A poem that sthpeakth for itsthelf!

Redundant (p. 92)
An old man contemplates the trawler on which he used to work. The sight of it brings back memories of his working life and thoughts of what the future holds for them both.

REFLECTIONS

Back in the Playground Blues (p. 96)
Adrian Mitchell reflects that in the school playground it is the bully boys who hold sway, taking it out on whoever they can, and that it is nonsense for adults to suggest that being bullied does the victims good by preparing them for adult life.

Money (p. 97)
The American poet Carl Sandburg considers various ideas about what money is and what it can and can not buy.

Fantasy of an African Boy (p. 97)
This poem by James Berry won the Poetry Society's National Poetry Competition in 1981. An African boy thinks about the money which he and millions like him need so much and have not got, but which he knows is somewhere, if only those who have it would let it go.

Life Insurance (p. 98)
Edward Lowbury reflects on what you are actually being offered when you take out a life insurance policy. He suggests it is worth taking a second look at what the blurb (the advertising copy) appears to be offering.

The Unbeliever (p. 99)
The title of the poem is ironic. The term 'unbeliever' is usually used to describe a person who does not believe in God. The person in the poem is an unbeliever, because he rejects the view that mankind and the universe were created by

chance and that everything that exists can be explained scientifically.

Zen Legend (p. 100)

Zen is a movement within the Buddhist religion that stresses the practice of meditation as the means to enlightenment and an understanding of reality. Followers of Zen are helped in their search for enlightenment by a Zen master, but 'awareness' can not be taught. The master offers help, but the individual must discover enlightenment for himself.

The Not-So-Good Earth (p. 101)

This poem by the Australian poet Bruce Dawe is about how people react when they see film of appalling human suffering on TV. The family watching pictures of Chinese peasants starving are more concerned with adjusting the focus of the set than with the horrific scenes being shown on the screen. The pictures do not shock them, because they view them as part of another TV spectacle, in which there is even a commercial break for an advertisement for Craven A, a brand of cigarettes. The reference to 'Confucian analects' is to the sayings of the ancient Chinese philosopher, Confucius, which have been passed down through the centuries.

The Sensitive Philanthropist (p. 101)

A philanthropist is a person who does things in order to try to help fellow human beings. A sensitive person is someone who feels things deeply. Again, there is irony in the title. The poet writes about someone who feels human suffering so deeply that he would prefer not to be reminded of it. He offers money (baksheesh, which means a tip or gratuity) if it can be arranged so that he will not have to face up to the reality of suffering directly. We are left to reflect on the motives of those who donate money for the alleviation of suffering. Do they do so, like the man in the poem, in an attempt to shut out the terrible problems and to buy peace of mind?

Democracy (p. 102)

A plea for freedom and civil rights by the black American poet Langston Hughes. A poem that was first published in 1948.

A Wish (p. 103)

Another poem from Sipho Sepamla's *The Soweto I Love*. Atlas was a Greek god, who was supposed to hold up the pillars of the universe.

Index of Authors

Appleton, Peter 43
Aylen, Leo 23, 38, 66

Baynton, L. T. 2
Berry, James 4, 48, 50, 97
Bold, Alan 62, 63, 67

Carnegie, Debbie 7
Collinson, Laurence 74
Cook, Stanley 13, 15
Coulson, Stella 87
Crichton Smith, Iain 4, 22, 48, 50, 84, 92
Cuddling, Ripyard 91

D., Peter 40
Dağlarca, Fazil Hüsnü 70
Davidson, Joan 58
Dawe, Bruce 25, 101

Enright, D. J. 101

Flood, Sally 88

Gilbey, Alan 3
Glasgow, Alex 11

Harris, Milly 10
Harrison, Gregory 90
hoban, faye 79
Holman, Carl 76
Hughes, Langston 102
Hutchins, Liz 51

Jennings, Elizabeth 32

K., Alan 42
Kingsbury, R. 49
Kirkup, James 26, 80, 100
Kitching, John 6, 14, 31
Kizerman, Rudolph 17, 64

Landesman, Fran 2, 6
Lerner, Laurence 44
Lester, Julius 39
Lochhead, Liz 7
Lowbury, Edward 31, 98, 99
Lowery, Martyn 56

M., Paul 41
Magee, Wes 12, 16, 17, 24, 54, 77
McGough, Roger 36, 60
Milligan, Spike 8, 24
Mitchell, Adrian 33, 81, 96
Money, Alf 92
Morgan, Edwin 12, 30
Morgan, Robert 82

Owen, Gareth 28, 92

Palmer, Timothy 78
Perneki, Michael 71

Rand, Jimi 60, 68
Rive, Richard 70
Rosselson, Leon 84

S., Eddie 41
Sandburg, Carl 97
Scannell, Vernon 15, 36
Scott, Gary 80
Sepamla, Sipho 74, 103
Sillitoe, Alan 85
Simmons, James 76
Stevenson, Anne 25
Sutton, David 53

Vitez, Grigor 75
Voznesensky, Andrey 55

Walker, Ted 61
Watt, W. W. 22
Wevill, David 29
Williams, Frederick 37